ALL ALONG THE RHINE

Hippocrene is NUMBER ONE in International Cookbooks

Africa and Oceania
Best of Regional African Cooking
Egyptian Cooking
Good Food from Australia
Traditional South African Cookery
Taste of Eritrea

Asia and Near East
Afghan Food and Cookery
Best of Goan Cooking
Best of Kashmiri Cooking
Imperial Mongolian Cooking
The Joy of Chinese Cooking
The Art of South Indian Cooking
The Indian Spice Kitchen
The Art of Persian Cooking
The Art of Israeli Cooking
The Art of Turkish Cooking
The Art of Uzbek Cooking

Mediterranean
Best of Greek Cuisine
Taste of Malta
A Spanish Family Cookbook
Tastes of North Africa

Western Europe
Art of Dutch Cooking
Best of Austrian Cuisine
A Belgian Cookbook
Cooking in the French Fashion
    (bilingual)
Celtic Cookbook
Cuisines of Portuguese Encounters
English Royal Cookbook
The Swiss Cookbook
Traditional Recipes from Old England
The Art of Irish Cooking
Traditional Food from Scotland
Traditional Food from Wales
The Scottish-Irish Pub and Hearth
    Cookbook
A Treasury of Italian Cuisine (bilingual)

Scandinavia
Best of Scandinavian Cooking
The Best of Finnish Cooking
The Best of Smorgasbord Cooking
Good Food from Sweden

Central Europe
All Along the Rhine
All Along the Danube
Best of Albanian Cooking
Best of Croatian Cooking
Bavarian Cooking
Traditional Bulgarian Cooking
The Best of Czech Cooking
The Best of Slovak Cooking
The Art of Hungarian Cooking
Hungarian Cookbook
Art of Lithuanian Cooking
Polish Heritage Cookery
The Best of Polish Cooking
Old Warsaw Cookbook
Old Polish Traditions
Treasury of Polish Cuisine
    (bilingual)
Poland's Gourmet Cuisine
Taste of Romania
Taste of Latvia

Eastern Europe
The Cuisine of Armenia
The Best of Russian Cooking
Traditional Russian Cuisine
    (bilingual)
The Best of Ukrainian Cuisine

Americas
Argentina Cooks
Cooking the Caribbean Way
Mayan Cooking
The Honey Cookbook
The Art of Brazilian Cookery
The Art of South American Cookery
Old Havana Cookbook (bilingual)

All Along the Rhine

Recipes, Wines and Lore
from
Germany, France, Switzerland,
Austria, Liechtenstein, and Holland

Kay Shaw Nelson

Hippocrene Books, Inc.
New York

For information, address:
HIPPOCRENE BOOKS, INC.
171 Madison Avenue
New York, NY 10016

ISBN 0-7818-0830-8

Cataloging-in-Publication Data available from the Library of Congress.

Printed in the United States of America.

TO

RAE AND WAYNE

MY

RHINE RIVER

DINING AND TRAVELING

COMPANIONS

CONTENTS

ACKNOWLEDGMENTS

First, I wish to thank George Blagowidow and Carol Chitnis, the publisher and managing editor of Hippocrene Books, for suggesting that I write *All Along The Rhine*.

This includes a special thanks to Carol for her helpful guidance and suggestions throughout the writing of this book.

As always I wish to thank my daughter, Rae, for her journeys with me along the Rhine River and for her continual support and technical assistance while writing the book.

Over the years, many friends and acquaintances have helped me considerably in my quest for knowledge to produce a Rhine guide that is part history book, part travelogue, part cookbook. I thank them all, especially those who shared meals and visits to the Rhine countries during the time I lived in Frankfurt, Germany. Before and after then many friendly people in Alsace, Switzerland, Austria, and Holland as well as Liechtenstein provided hospitality, helpful talks, and recipes during my travels.

I wish to thank particularly the Austrian and Swiss Tourist Boards and the Liechtenstein National Tourist Office for their valuable information and guidance.

Photo credits:

Pages 47 and 52: Courtesy of Liechtenstein Press and Information Office.
Pages 75 and 99: Courtesy of the Austrian National Tourist Office.
Pages 111 and 142: Courtesy of the German National Tourist Office.
Pages 145, 152, and 165: Courtesy of the French Government Tourist Office.
Pages 183, 189, and 204: Courtesy of the Netherlands Board of Tourism.

The Rhine

PREFACE

It was a glorious crisp autumn day in Strasbourg, a charming and exquisitely preserved Rhine city that maintains a look of the Middle Ages but is one of Europe's outstanding cultural and commerce centers. Traveling with my husband, who was introducing me to his favorite Continental locales, we enjoyed the historic monuments, culinary specialties, and local wines of delightful Alsace, a bountiful province in northeastern France. It's a rewarding place to visit for dining and drinking experiences.

I became enchanted with the region's rugged scenery, hospitable people, gingerbread architecture, rolling fertile fields and, especially, the atmospheric restaurants serving gastronomic masterpieces, some of the most interesting and varied in France. The regional cuisine has many noteworthy specialties ranging from quiches and *foie gras* (goose liver), and the flavorful sauerkraut dish called *choucroute garnie* to flaky apple tarts, smothered in rich cream, and plum cakes. I still recall the compatibility of the marvelous food and wine.

Here also was my first view of the mighty Rhine that borders Strasbourg, a great river port and ancient free city with a proud tradition. Only the legendary waterway separates Germany from Alsace, a region that often looks German but is passionately French, noted for its distinctive hospitality. It is not difficult to imagine why the two countries have fought over this jewel on the Ill River, a tributary of the Rhine that joins the larger body of water just northeast of Strasbourg, for so long. Or why the city is a stunning synthesis of French-German architecture, culture, language, music, and gastronomy.

Something happened that day in Alsace, something that made me want to see and experience the Rhine which I had thought of almost exclusively as a German river, though it rises in Switzerland, flows along Liechtenstein and Austria, and reaches the sea in the Netherlands. Imbued with a basic sense of curiosity and a love of adventure and good fare, I wanted to visit all the Rhine countries and taste their foods, dishes, and drinks, especially the wines. For I realized that the river's surrounding lands, made up of combinations of cultures associated with the waterway, would prove to be a marvelous gastronomic journey. I was at an incomparable crossroads. But then my idea was only a hope or a dream.

In Strasbourg we began our city tour with a visit to the towering rose-colored Cathedral Notre Dame, a marvel of Gothic design renowned for its stained-glass windows, remarkable statues, and 470-foot spire that seems to beckon everyone. Its wonderfully macabre astronomical clock, however, is the major attraction. At noon just about everyone stops by to view its parade of wooden figures that include one of Christ chasing the image of Death, the Apostles, and even a cock's crow greeting the appearance of St. Peter.

Soon thereafter we were dining at the Maison Kammerzell, a restored, intricately carved, timbered fifteenth-century house that has a glorious setting and distinguished surroundings, facing the cathedral. It's still a popular restaurant specializing in typical Alsatian cooking. We found the dark-paneled bar to be ideal for enjoying a glass of chilled spicy Gewürztraminer and goblets of dry Riesling wines with wedges of a tasty onion tart and creamy Munster cheese. Then came a sublime *choucroute* flavored with juniper berries, apples, and wine, and garnished with a variety of smoked meats.

Meanwhile, my husband was explaining more about the complicated and sad past of the city and region, once a part of the Holy Roman Empire that had been fought over between Germany and France until 1944 when the Allied Forces liberated the region and it became French again. And that evening, while being honored with a dinner given by some of his friends, I heard more about Alsace's heroic history and acquired a lasting admiration for the determined Alsatians and their patriotism. As one of the men reminded me, Strasbourg was where Roger de Lisle wrote "La Marseillaise," France's national anthem, in 1722.

Whenever I think if Strasbourg, I picture this wonderful day and evening, packed full of one inspirational event after another. Fortunately, as luck would have it, I was destined to return several times to this city and region. Later, we had the great fortune to live three years in Frankfurt, Germany, and from there I was able to explore and enjoy the Rhine River nations.

Straddling the Main River just before it meets the Rhine, Frankfurt, sometimes known as Frankfort on the Main (pronounced "Mine"), was and is a thriving financial capital and cultural center. It's also an important transportation hub with one of the world's busiest airports, the gateway by air to Germany and to Central Europe. Among its historical treasures is Goethe's House and Museum, the birthplace of the poet Johann W. Goethe, several museums, the site of Gutenberg's print shop, and the *Romer*, (town hall), noted for its *Kaiserssal* (Imperial Hall), the scene of the coronation banquet of ten German Emperors.

Lying on the Rhine-Main basin, the city has been a center of civilization since time immemorial. After the Romans built a bridge over the Main, the nearby settlement was called "Franks' ford." As a thriving marketplace and crossroads, it soon became a place of considerable importance.

Although the city has a good range of distinctive dining places, I sought out the neighborhood Gasthofs, taverns serving an assortment of wursts, or sausages, including the frankfurter. Still popular with visitors are the traditional eating places in the old quarter of Sachsenhausen on the south bank of the Main, home of the famous *Ebbelwein* (apple wine) taverns. Here we usually ordered the wine, a rather hard cider, and *Handkäs mit Musik*, soft cheese served with raw onions, oil, and vinegar, to spread on dark bread, plus hearty meat hot pots.

One of Frankfurt's great advantages is its central location. We could travel by car, boat, sometimes by train, to all the neighboring Rhine River countries, from Switzerland to the Netherlands. During our residence in Frankfurt, I frequently went in all seasons on the river, and along its banks, enjoying all elements of the enchanting landscape— rich architecture, historic towns and cities, castles, and vineyards— attempting to capture its fascinating past and present vitality. I always had ample time to savor the wealth of culinary specialties.

It is not surprising that Americans and other travelers find the cuisines of each Rhine nation interesting to explore. For the pleasures of the table are ever present and ever rewarding. The art of cookery flourishes no less creatively in provincial hideaways than in renowned cities, to the delight of both the knowledgeable native and the enterprising tourist.

Over the centuries each of these nations has developed a distinctive and individual cuisine. In a few cases, regional similarities may exist, but never sameness. None of these countries is vast in territory, but each has made maximum use of the products of the field, forest, river, and stream. Born of national pride or necessity, culinary treasures have been created in royal palace or humble home and evolved against the checkered background of European history.

For me, today, as before, the Rhine culinary treats are numerous and to savor them is always a great experience. One soon finds that the cookery has a special place in the culture and, like the charming towns, lovely landscapes, and idyllic attractions, reflects the happiness and creativity of the people. While traveling anywhere in the Rhine locales, one is constantly lured to the table by culinary temptations. For a love of good dining has long been an important aspect of everyday living.

INTRODUCTION

The broad, swift flowing Rhine River, Europe's most important inland waterway, has been attracting explorers, warriors, and travelers for centuries. Today it is more popular than ever, welcoming tourists from around the world. The incredibly busy and scenic legendary river has a fleet of handsome steamers offering a variety of outstanding journeys. My fondest recollections of the Rhine River countries are, however, those enjoyed by car, driving leisurely and often up one side and down the other, stopping to view and savor all the numerous delights, including joyous seasonal fetes and festivals. Even the train offers rewarding glimpses of the river's enthralling sights that change dramatically from season to season.

Cradle of European art, culture, history, and folklore for thousands of years, the Rhine River has an interest for everyone along its verdant shores. It's an intriguing tale of romance and tragedy, legend and myth, and good-natured hospitality, alluring architecture, literature and music fans, history buffs, wine connoisseurs, and gastronomes. Travelers are smitten by the spectacular vistas of the river, winding through and past great contrasting scenery, while stopping at celebrated cities and cozy villages.

They love to discover the Old World enchantment of the fascinating places along the famous waterway. There is the elation, the joyousness, the exuberance, the daring that led men to make it a path of exploration and a crossroads of history. Little wonder that the Rhine has been enshrined in the literature and music of its lands, waxing rhapsodic about its mythical charms.

For me, the Rhine means much more than delightful landscapes, picturesque old towns and age-old attractions. It's a reminder of all the adventures and good times I experienced while learning about and enjoying local foods, dishes, and libations. Traveling to and in the Rhine countries enabled me to enjoy the versatility of the diverse gastronomic pleasures. The cookery is as fascinating to explore as it is rewarding to savor. To dine in such lovely historic places is always a joyous occasion.

The Rhine River region, varying in soil, climate, and terrain, has a complex history comprising invasion and conquest, the influence of religious affiliation, and the effects of political and social orientation or allegiance, sometimes dictated by circumstances or royal decree. In earliest times Germanic and Celtic tribes settled along the river's banks, and Celts sent their wares up the Rhine. They are believed to have given the Rhine its name. Today there are still several Celtic place names in France and Germany.

The Romans maintained a Rhine fleet, and to stop interference in Gaul, Julius Caesar built his famous bridge over the river near Andernach in the summer of 55 B.C., marking Rome's first penetration into Germany. For centuries before and after, tribes, races, and great powers crossed and recrossed the Rhine and fought for its important settlements. Today no other river has so many old and famous cities on its bank. Yet, the region has never been politically united and each nation maintains its individual government and culture.

Fed by alpine springs, the mighty Rhine flows about 850 miles from its origin in southeast Switzerland, then along Liechtenstein and Austria, through the French Alps, western Germany, and the Netherlands into the North Sea. No European river varies more in character throughout its course than the Rhine, called "Rhein" in German, "Rhin" in French, and "Rijn" in Dutch, names that all derived from the Latin "Rhenus."

To trace the course of the river from its origins in the Swiss Alps is an enlightening journey. It begins with the Upper Rhine that rises in two principal glacier-fed head streams, the Vorderrhein and the Hinterrhein, uniting to form the Rhine near Chur. Sitting in a deep valley amidst the charm of Heidi country, this attractive city is the regional capital and the oldest continuously settled place in Switzerland. Then the river leaves the Alps, plunging down to a broad valley to form the boundary first between Switzerland and Liechtenstein, and then flowing north, between Switzerland and Austria. This beautiful stretch passes by orchards, gardens, and neat cottages before entering the enormous Bodensee, or Lake Constance.

Leaving the lake at its western end, the river tumbles over the spectacular Rhinefall, a dramatic series of falls near the old Rhine city of Schaffhausen, and from there defines the Swiss-German frontier into Basel, a fun-loving medieval center and Renaissance city.

Below Basel, the Rhine turns abruptly northward, flowing across a broad valley bounded by Germany's Black Forest on the east and Alsace's Vosges Mountains on the west. For much of this distance the river is the boundary between Germany and France, and along its way is joined by the Ill River as its main French tributary, and the Neckar at Mannheim and Main at Mainz from the German side.

North of Mainz, the river turns directly westward, and then at Bingen, it widens and swings north into the Middle Rhine, a spectacular 90-mile gorge sometimes called the "heroic" Rhine, because of the legends associated with it. One of Europe's major tourist attractions renowned for its terraced vineyards, steep wooded hills, ruined castles, and dramatic scenery, it has been celebrated through the ages by artists in paintings, music, poetry, and myth. Here is the famous Loreley or Lorelie Rock, descending almost perpendicular to the water. Legend has it that the rock was once a beautiful nymph, clothed in white with a wreath of stars in her flowing hair. She used to sit and sing sweet songs, luring boatmen to their destruction with her music. The Loreley has vanished but her charm lives on.

At Remagen the Lower Rhine widens, crossing the plain of northwest Germany, passing the cities of Cologne, Düsseldorf, and Duisburg on its journey to the Netherlands. There it divides into three main streams: the Waal, the Lek, and the Ijssel, to flow past Arnhem and Rotterdam to reach the North Sea at the Hook of Holland. Previously, before the river's course was shifted to the south, it entered the sea near The Hague.

Over the centuries difficult river passages and rapids have been brought under control and its navigability has been increased by the building of canals. An international waterway since the Treaty of Vienna in 1815, the Rhine is navigable as far south as the Rhine falls on the Swiss-German border.

It was from the Romans, who for centuries ruled a great part of the Rhine lands, that the people learned the fundamentals of agriculture, viniculture, animal husbandry, cooking, and dining. It is believed, however, that the Italians, wishing to monopolize the wine trade, at one time forbade the making of wine. But their efforts failed. Today Germany's Rhinegau and France's Alsace are world-famous for their wines, and Austria, Switzerland, and Liechtenstein all have notable wines as well as numerous other unique drinks.

During the Dark Ages, it was in the monasteries, the only places of tranquility in those turbulent times, that the arts bequeathed by the Romans were preserved. The monks cultivated herb and vegetable gardens, as well as orchards and vineyards, and had special rooms for baking, brewing, and preserving. From their grapes and fruits were made their highly prized wines and liqueurs.

With the growth of permanent Rhine settlements and more variety in food as well as drinks was provided, seasonal fairs and markets were set up at strategic crossroad cities. As workers and their masters gathered, often from considerable distances, merchants displayed and sold their wares, minstrels entertained, and everyone made merry with feasting and drinking. These profitable and convivial events developed over the years into fabulous fairs still celebrated with great gusto throughout the Rhine countries.

From earliest times the Rhine people were guided by the forces of nature for their daily living, seasonal celebrations, and family beliefs. Planting, harvesting, and feast days acquired certain meaningful rites and practices. As Christianity spread throughout the area, many of the pagan customs and festivals were adopted by the new religion for holidays that are still observed in the European nations. Each Rhine country has its own festive days with traditional foods, drinks, and folkways. For cooking and dining customs have been handed down from one generation to the next, and are still cherished in homes of the Rhine countries.

In this representative collection of traditional and contemporary Rhine recipes may be found a wealth of culinary treasures carefully evolved over the centuries by creative cooks. Because the cookery is derived from a jigsaw puzzle of peoples, customs and foods, there are some exotic and exciting contrasts. Indeed, the kitchens of these countries have produced some of the world's most cherished delicacies, as well as flavorful, down-to-earth hearty dishes that have enduring appeal. Such gastronomic specialties, which are easy and rewarding to prepare, are intriguing additions to the culinary repertoire, either for everyday dining or for special occasions.

For all their national differences, or perhaps because of them, the cookery of the Rhine countries is enjoyable, colorful, and delectable. In this book I present a wide range of regional recipes with notes of native foods, dining customs, and places and sometimes, people associated with them. It's dedicated to the intrepid traveler, the adventurous cook, and to all those who want to enhance their understanding of good food and find joy in eating dishes that are unusual and appealing.

Learning about a country's food and drinks is an engaging way to find out about a land and its people. Hopefully, these recipes will bring to readers the pleasure and sheer goodness that the Rhine culinary repertoire deserves.

SWITZERLAND

Heidi Country, Cheeses and Chocolate

View of the Rhine in Basel, Switzerland.

The first time I visited Switzerland it was a whirlwind visit to the beautiful, hospitable small country during a trip from northern Italy to eastern France. It didn't take long to become enchanted with the contrasting spectacular scenery, from deep green valleys to towering ice-capped mountains, and the attractions of cosmopolitan Geneva and aristocratic Neuchâtel. We drove through immaculate villages with half-timbered chalets and flower-filled window boxes, and stopped at pleasing restaurants to enjoy the national culinary specialties and wines. As one always dines well in Switzerland, I came away with many gastronomic memories.

Over the years I've returned several times to this charming country in the heart of Europe where three cultures meet and where four different languages (German, French, Italian, and Romansch) are spoken. A visit to Switzerland is a stimulating experience at any season and for any reason. Whether enjoying exhilarating winter sports, relaxing beside a placid lake, or simply viewing the ever-present scenic mountain panorama, I delight in exploring the indigenous cooking, some of the dishes familiar and others vaguely known. Each meal proves to be a rewarding adventure. Choosing a regional specialty is full of diverse surprises and delights.

Swiss cookery, like the language and culture, has been influenced extensively by its neighbors. Thus there are many dishes resembling those of Germany, France and Italy. But the traditional independence of the nation and its people is reflected in the specialties of each valley and town that were created long ago by inventive thrifty cooks who shared a deep passion for nourishing good fare. Fortunately, they always have been blessed with the best and freshest of ingredients, readily available from productive farmlands and well-tended animals and poultry. Outstanding among the renowned Swiss foods are dairy products, garden-fresh vegetables, flavorful honey, rich fruits, and excellent meats, particularly pork and veal, as well as game and poultry. Housewives shop daily for whatever they need at attractive markets and bake a wide range of breads, cakes, fruit tarts, and pastries.

I enjoyed many of the innovative local dishes during a memorable Swiss culinary adventure after a weekend in Davos, a noted winter resort in the culturally diverse southeastern canton, or state, called the "Grisons" in French, "Graubünden" in German, and "Grigoni" in Italian. It's often spoken of as "Switzerland in miniature." Here my husband and I decided to leave the attractions of the Alps and cities and drive through the cantons dominated by the Rhine River. We began in the lovely Engadine Valley with its surprisingly undiscovered mountain villages and countryside, and then journeyed through an alluring terrain, ranging from flat farmlands to alpine foothills, scattered with culturally rich towns and quaint farming communities. Here traditional eating and sumptuous feasts are still a way of life. And, as a Swiss friend told me, the inhabitants are some of the best hosts in the country and the food is quite different from that of other regions. My Swiss friend was right.

As we soon discovered, the Grisons, a canton bordering Austria and Liechtenstein in the north and, in the east and south, Italy, has its own distinct personality and charm. The history, however, centers around its many mountain passes which brought advantages as well as invaders and conquerors from neighboring lands to the region. Eventually the area became free and in 1803 was incorporated in Switzerland as the eighteenth canton. The Grisons is also famous for its rivers which flow north, south, and east into the North Sea, the Adriatic, and the Black Sea. Here the Rhine rises. Two glacier-fed torrents, the Vorder Rhine and Hinter Rhine, flow eastward in the high Alps to form their union near Chur. The proud people of the countryside cherish their charming gabled houses, rural way of life, and carefully preserve their cultural heritage, including colorful festivals and country cooking.

To our delight, we began our Rhine journey in Chur, the region's capital that sits in a deep valley carved by the Rhine. Now a modern city its origins go back to the Romans who founded Curia Rhaetorum south of the river and on a route that led to Lake Constance. In its preserved historic heart, Old Town, museums, massive stone houses, domed belfries, the *Rathaus* (town hall) and centerpiece cathedral, all bear traces of the city's Latin and German past. Also of interest are a few restaurants serving regional specialties and wines.

Our choice for dinner, however, was the dining room in the historic Romantik Hotel Stern built in 1677. Known for its imaginative Grisons decor, art, and cuisine, the hotel has authentic regional dishes served with wine in pewter pitchers by waitresses in folk costume. Its ambiance is warm and welcoming.

Today when I think of Chur, I recall the unusual cured meats, ranging from sausages to smoked bacon and especially the highly prized *Bündnerfleisch,* paper-thin slices of beef that have been dried in the mountain air. The Swiss enjoy it as an appetizer, served with crusty dark bread and perhaps dried apples and pears, with a glass of local Veltliner wine. The beef is also eaten with potato salad. Other superb meats include *salsiz,* a hard salami sausage, and *beinwust,* so named because it is made with crushed marrowbone. Ragouts of all kinds are also popular in the area, and so are venison and young goat, *gitzi,* in season. *Maluns,* a fried-potato dish, accompanied by cheese and applesauce, and versions of Italian gnocchi, is typical supper fare.

The pastry cooks of the Grisons are known internationally for their cakes, fruit tarts such as *engadiner nusstort* (walnut tart), crusty breads, and a special long, oval cake called *birnbrot,* pear bread, made from rolling a bread-like mixture around a paste consisting of pears, nuts, raisins, and spices. Served in thin, buttered slices, I enjoyed the cake for dessert but also with tea or hot chocolate as an afternoon treat.

Later, driving north through the Rhine River valley we stopped at the charming spa town of Bad Ragaz that is known for its therapeutic thermal waters which have attracted health-seekers for centuries. Anyone who has read the beloved story of *Heidi* by Johanna Spyri knows that this is the place where Clara, her crippled friend, came to "take the cure" for paralysis. Now visitors to the thriving resort can enjoy the healthful waters, play golf, take a cable car to the high mountains, or visit Tamina Gorge, the source of the thermal springs. On a special tour to the nearby village of Maienfeld, full of fountains and vineyards, one can trace the footsteps of Heidi and her companions by hiking from the Heidihof Hotel up to the spectacular mountain locales that inspired the book.

Following the Swiss Rhineland through cantons bordered on the north by Germany and the east by Austria and dominated by the great river, is a wonderful journey with a melange of attractions. We drove through St. Gallen, famous for its lace, embroidery, and fruit; Thurgau, a rich farming area along Lake Constance; and Schaffhausen, associated especially with the Rhinefalls or Rhine Falls, the most famous waterfall in Europe. Stein-am-Rhein, a preserved medieval village with a main street of houses painted with murals depicting the history of the home or its occupants, is at the point where the Rhine leaves the legendary lake. Here we dined on delicious trout, caught fresh from the Rhine, at a small inn on the waterfront promenade. Then after a drive across the canton of Glarus, a productive dairy land, we arrived at Basel, once a Roman fort and now an international city but still reminiscent of an old imperial town.

Known throughout the centuries as a cultural and education center, it's famed for native philosophers, painters, and mathematicians. Located astride the Rhine River, at the juncture of France and Germany, Basel's history, dating back to the Celts and Romans, has evolved around its strategic location. On the northern bank of the Rhine is Kleinbasel (Little Basel), surrounded by German territory, and on the south lies Grossbasel (Large Basel) with its Old Town and cathedral, *Rathaus*, art galleries, museums, and market place selling fruit, vegetables, and fish.

I always enjoy the city's Old-World charm, preserved medieval buildings, zoo, colorful annual carnival, and old-fashioned German-style cooking served in comfortable wine houses or cafés. Here one dines on substantial soups including dumplings or meatballs, fine hams and sausages, and game dishes. But there are also excellent specialties made with fish, especially salmon from the Rhine, small cheesecakes, and *basler leckerli*, a spice-honey cookie. Basel is also famous for its cherries from which the local kirsch is made.

The city has, of course, sophisticated dining places with French-inspired dishes as well as German and Swiss creations. Of them all, the most notable establishment is the Hotel Drei Konige, or Three Kings, said to be the oldest inn in Switzerland, dating from 1026. Located directly on the banks of the Rhine River, it was originally called *Zur Blume*, meaning "At the Flower." Its present name, however, derives from a historic meeting between three kings: Conrad II, emperor of the Holy Roman Empire; his son, later known as Henry III; and Rudolf III, the last king of Burgundy. At their meeting a treaty was drawn up for the transference of territories which are now western Switzerland and southern France.

Whether dining in informal *stubli* (pubs), charming country inns, or grand restaurants, it's always a memorable experience. One is sure to find delectable dishes. Swiss cookery reflects not only devotion to national tradition but also creative assimilation and adaptation of foreign influences. The following selection of traditional and representative recipes offers an appealing introduction to a captivating cuisine that has particular variety in the Rhine regions.

SWISS CHEESES

Since ancient times Switzerland has been known for its incomparable rustic and full-flavored cheeses made in a land where milk, cream, and butter form an important part of the cuisine. Julius Caesar ordered that Swiss cheeses be sent to him from over the Alps to Rome. For centuries the making of cheese has been an important village industry and a large part of the Swiss culture. Today it is a regionally controlled, cooperative effort with each area specializing in its own type of cheese.

What most people outside the country think of as "Swiss" cheese are the flavorful large, dense-textured kinds with big holes or eyes that were made originally by "mountain people." Doubtless the greatest and best known is Emmental (EM-awn-TAHL) that originated in the lovely green and rolling valley of the Emme River in the canton of Bern. The largest of the Swiss cheeses, it is easily recognized by its large holes, dry and hard rind, light golden color, and sweet, nutty flavor. The mainstay of any tray of selected cheeses, it is ideal for fondue, sandwiches, and salads, as well as omelets and baked dishes. It also marries well with fruit and wine. Gruyère, named for the perfectly preserved medieval town of Gruyères, is not as large, has smaller holes and a pleasant assertive fruity flavor. Because it melts easily and is smooth, it is an excellent cheese for fondue, soups, and grilled cheese sandwiches. Its distinctive flavor also goes well with fruit.

Another excellent cheese, Appenzeller, or Appenzell, derives its name from a small canton in northeastern Switzerland. The rind and curd are golden yellow, and the unique fruity or spicy tang comes from a special mixture of pepper, herbs, white wine, or cider. It is a fine eating cheese and goes well with fruit and red wine. It's also perfect for fondue and salads as well as baked potatoes and potato dishes. Sbrinz, the hardest and oldest Swiss cheese without any holes, is excellent for grating. It's especially good in soups and sauces and is often cut in very thin slices to eat with bread. Other excellent cheeses include Raclette, used principally for preparing a dish of the same name; Vacherin, a variant of Gruyère; and Tête de Moine, with a strong fruity flavor and aroma.

Cheeses, of course, are often eaten uncooked, either plain or with other foods. In Switzerland the local cheeses are standard breakfast foods, as well as common snacks and desserts. The repertoire of cheese dishes includes sandwiches, omelets, souffles, soups, salads, and pies.

SCHAFFHAUSEN CHEESE-ONION TART

This savory tart, now popular throughout Switzerland, originated in the canton of Schaffhausen. Its capital, the ancient Rhine city of the same name and gateway to Switzerland from Germany, is a famous town on Lake Constance. Once an important transshipping station for river cargoes, interrupted by the Rhine Falls, it is picturesquely situated on the right bank of the river. The name is said to derive from that of the skiff houses along the riverbank. Today it's known for its medieval buildings, with painted façades and quaint projecting windows called *oriel*, typical of early alpine architecture. Also, there's the Rheinhotel Fischerzunft, an exceptional hostelry for fine dining with an ideal location on the pedestrian promenade running along the Rhine. From it one can take boat rides along the river, trips to the Rhine Falls, and to Stein-am-Rhein. Here is my recipe for the tart.

Pastry for one 9-inch pie
3 tablespoons unsalted butter
3 large yellow onions, peeled and thinly sliced
1 tablespoon all-purpose flour
2 cups cream or milk
4 large eggs, beaten
2 cups grated Emmental or Swiss cheese
Salt, freshly ground pepper

Preheat oven to 375 degrees. Fit prepared crust into a pie pan.

In a medium skillet melt butter over medium-high heat. Add onion slices; sauté until translucent, about 7 minutes. Stir in flour and 1 cup cream or milk. Cook, stirring, for 1 minute. Turn into a large bowl. Add the remaining 1 cup cream or milk, beaten eggs, and grated cheese. Season with salt and pepper. Mix well. Turn into prepared pie shell, spreading evenly. Bake until filling is set in the center and is golden brown in spots, about 45 minutes. Remove from oven and cool on a wire rack. Serve warm or at room temperature. 6 servings.

CARNIVAL FLOUR SOUP

The Swiss love soups that they make in great variety and enjoy for all meals and as snacks. Because they are practical people, they prepare some of their traditional soups with only a few simple ingredients. One of their favorites is *mehlsuppe*, based on flour and butter, and seasoned variously. While eaten throughout the year, it is particularly associated with the famous *Fasnacht*, or carnival celebration, in Basel. There everyone turns out for a spirited lantern parade beginning at 4 A.M., the Monday morning after Ash Wednesday, to start the festivities with the playing of fifes and drums and pealing of bells. At dawn it is the tradition to eat flour soup and onion pie. Thus fortified, the celebrants can report for a morning's work and then commence merrymaking all over again in the afternoon.

5 tablespoons unsalted butter
5 tablespoons all-purpose flour
6 cups hot beef bouillon or water
1 medium yellow onion stuck with 4 cloves
1 bay leaf
Salt
1½ cups stale bread croutons
½ cup grated Gruyère or Swiss cheese

In a large saucepan melt the butter over medium-high heat. Stir in flour. Cook, stirring, until mixture is smooth and deep brown, but not burned. Remove from the stove. Add hot bouillon, stirring until smooth. Add onion with the cloves and bay leaf. Season with salt. Return to the stove. Reduce heat to medium-low. Cook, covered, stirring occasionally, for 1 hour. Remove from the stove. Remove and discard onion and bay leaf. Serve with the croutons floating on the surface and sprinkled with the cheese. 6 servings.

MUSHROOM BOUILLON

One of the most popular foods in Switzerland is the mushroom. Both wild and cultivated varieties are used extensively in the various dishes, including soups. This simple, yet refreshing, bouillon is excellent as a first course for luncheon or dinner.

¾ pound fresh mushrooms
8 cups beef bouillon
1 cup dry sherry
Freshly ground pepper
⅓ cup minced scallions, with some green tops

Wash mushrooms to remove any dirt. Cut off any tough stem ends. Slice thickly lengthwise through the caps. In a large saucepan combine mushrooms and bouillon over medium-high heat. Bring to a boil. Reduce heat to medium-low. Cook, covered, for 10 minutes. Add sherry. Season with pepper. Heat 2 minutes. Serve garnished with scallions. 8 servings.

ALTDORF ONION-CHEESE SOUP

This easy-to-prepare soup is made with two favorite Swiss foods: onions and cheese. It's named for Altdorf, the capital of the canton of Uri and setting for William Tell's famous shooting of an apple from his young son's head. In the village's central square is an imposing statue of the large, bearded warrior-hero with a crossbow on his shoulder, and a small boy at his side.

6 medium yellow onions, peeled and sliced
6 tablespoons unsalted butter
8 cups beef bouillon
2 cups grated Emmental or Gruyère cheese
⅛ teaspoon freshly grated nutmeg
Salt, freshly ground pepper
6 slices toasted crusty white bread

Separate onion slices. In a large saucepan melt butter over medium-high heat. Add onion slices; sauté until translucent, about 8 minutes. Pour in bouillon; bring to a boil. Reduce heat to medium-low. Stir in 1½ cups of cheese. Add nutmeg. Season with salt and pepper. Cook, covered, until the cheese melts, about 15 minutes. To serve, spoon the soup into 6 bowls. Top each serving with a slice of toasted bread. Sprinkle with remaining ½ cup cheese. 6 servings.

CROQUE MONSIEUR

The Swiss are fond of this French-inspired hot sandwich that is made in several variations and served as a light entrée or snack.

4 slices buttered firm white bread
4 thin slices cooked ham
4 slices Emmental or Gruyère cheese
4 eggs, fried and kept warm
Preheat oven broiler.

Cover each slice of buttered bread with a slice of ham and cheese. Place in an ovenproof dish. To cook, place under preheated broiler until cheese is bubbly and melted, a few minutes. Top each sandwich with a hot egg; serve at once. 4 servings.

CHEESE FONDUE

Fondue, a gently bubbling pot of flavorful cheese into which one dips pieces of crusty bread, is a festive Swiss specialty that has become popular around the world. The name comes from the French verb *fondre*, meaning "to melt." Although its origins are not known, some persons say that fondue was created by mountain villagers who softened pieces of hardened cheese with a little wine in a pot over an open fire. Particularly appealing is the idea of do-it-yourself cookery, as the dish is placed in the middle of the table and the participants dunk bread cubes in a previously prepared aromatic creamy cheese mixture. The Swiss make fondue in a heavy flat-bottomed round dish with a handle which is called a *caquelon*. It can be earthenware or made of cast iron or other metal, but it has to be heavy to hold the heat. Possible substitutes are chafing dishes or casseroles. The dish is placed over heat such as a spirit-burner, candle, or other device that can be regulated while cooking. Also necessary are long-handled forks for spearing and dunking the bread cubes. Each piece of the bread should have some crust on it so it will not slip off the fork. (If this happens, the loser of the bread must forfeit a bottle of wine or kiss the person to his or her right.) Wine is very important to the dish; it should be a dry white one with enough acid to help liquefy the cheese. Good Swiss wines are Fendant-Pétillant or Neuchâtel.

The choice of cheese is of utmost significance, for in order to achieve the proper consistency and not lump or become stringy, it should be well matured. Usually it features a mix of Emmental and Gruyère, but variations use other Swiss cheeses such as Vacherin or Appenzeller. The preferred drink to serve with fondue is kirsch; or you may serve the same kind of wine that was used in the dish. Generally speaking, it is best not to serve very cold or chilled drinks with the fondue. In Switzerland a course of smoked meats, followed by fresh fruit and tea, is served after this cheese dish. This recipe is for the traditional Neuchâtel fondue, which I first enjoyed in that lovely Swiss city.

1 garlic clove, cut in half
2 cups dry white wine
1 or 2 teaspoons fresh lemon juice (optional)
½ pound (2 cups) Emmental cheese, diced or shredded
½ pound (2 cups) Gruyère cheese, diced or shredded
1 tablespoon cornstarch
3 tablespoons kirsch, gin, or vodka
⅛ teaspoon grated nutmeg
Salt, freshly ground pepper
About 8 slices crusty white bread, cut into cubes

Rub inside of a fondue dish or casserole with the garlic clove. Add wine and lemon juice, if used. Heat gradually over a low flame until the liquid begins to bubble. Gradually add cheeses, stirring constantly with a wooden spoon, until they melt. Dissolve cornstarch in the kirsch, gin or vodka; stir into cheese mixture. Increase the heat to moderate. Continue cooking and stirring until mixture is smooth and creamy. Add nutmeg. Season with salt and pepper. Keep bubbling over low heat while serving. To cook, each person spears a small piece of bread with a long-handled fork and then dips it into the cheese mixture before eating. 4 servings.

If the mixture becomes too thick while cooking, gradually add some warm wine to it, stirring as you do so, until it reaches the desired consistency.

MAIENFELD *RACLETTE*

*"**F**rom the old and pleasantly situated village of Maienfeld, a foot-path winds through green and shady meadows to the foot of the mountains, which on this side look down from their stern and lofty heights upon the valley below. The land grows gradually wilder as the path ascends, and the climber has not gone far before he begins to inhale the fragrance of the short grass and sturdy mountain-plants, for the way is steep and leads directly up to the summits above."*

— Introduction to *Heidi*.

Raclette, a traditional country dish immortalized in *Heidi* when her grandfather made it by scraping melted cheese for supper in front of an open hearth, is said to be from the canton of Valais. Here mountaineers invented the dish when, after a long day in the brisk air, they built bonfires for warmth and roasted their cheese before them. The name derives from the French verb *racler*, meaning "to scrape." Originally the dish was made in homes by holding or putting a large piece of cheese in front of an open fire and, as the cheese melted, scraping the soft surface onto a warm plate. It was then eaten with boiled potatoes in their skins and small pickled onions, gherkins, and freshly ground pepper. Now known all over Switzerland, *raclette* is made in Swiss homes and restaurants in a special electric grill. But it's more fun to enjoy it the old-fashioned way, at an open fire. The preferred cheeses from Valais are the semi-firm kinds that melt easily: Gomser, Bagnes, or Raclette. The recommended wine to serve with this dish is a chilled Valais Fendant. I recall first sampling *raclette* in an informal upstairs restaurant in a hostelry where the atmosphere was lightened with genial conversation sparked by lively interest in the preparation, service, and eating of the inviting dish. It is a specialty that promotes conviviality.

The Swiss have improvised a substitute plan for anyone wishing to make *raclette* in the home, where an open fire or electric grill are not available. Preheat oven to 450 degrees. Place a large piece of cheese or two or three thick slices in an ovenproof dish. When it begins to melt, scrape the cheese. Serve immediately on hot plates with the accompaniments mentioned above. Dark, crusty bread also goes well with the dish.

Basel, Switzerland.

BASEL SALMON WITH ONIONS

The favorite fish in Switzerland's port city of Basel has long been fresh salmon caught in the Rhine River. Once it was the custom to give one of the highly prized fish as a gift to a visiting dignitary. Today, visitors to the inviting city can dine on salmon in any of the excellent restaurants. This is the traditional way of preparing it.

9 tablespoons unsalted butter
2 medium yellow onions, peeled and thinly sliced
4 salmon steaks, about 1 inch thick
Salt, freshly ground pepper
All-purpose flour
½ cup dry white wine
⅓ cup chopped fresh parsley
1 large lemon, sliced

In a medium skillet melt 3 tablespoons of butter over medium-high heat. Add onions; sauté until translucent, about 5 minutes. Remove from heat; keep warm. Meanwhile, sprinkle salmon steaks with salt and pepper; dredge each one on both sides with flour.

In a large skillet melt the remaining 6 tablespoons of butter over medium-high heat. Add the salmon. Pan-fry gently until fork-tender, about 10 minutes. Remove to a platter and keep warm. Spoon sautéed onions over the salmon. Pour the wine into pan drippings. Scrape with a fork; bring quickly to a boil. Pour over the salmon. Sprinkle with parsley. Serve garnished with lemon slices. 4 servings.

MEATBALLS IN CHEESE SAUCE

Flavorful ground meat mixtures, made from ground pork or veal, or a combination of the two, that generally include piquant flavorings, have been traditional dishes in Switzerland for centuries. This specialty features meatballs cooked in a white–wine cheese sauce. Serve for a company luncheon or dinner.

1 pound ground pork
¾ pound ground cooked smoked ham
1¼ cups cracker crumbs
½ cup milk
1 egg
1 medium yellow onion, peeled and minced
2 teaspoons Worcestershire sauce
½ teaspoon dried marjoram
Salt, freshly ground pepper
2 tablespoons unsalted butter
2 cups dry white wine
1 cup grated Swiss cheese

In a large bowl thoroughly combine the ground pork and ham, cracker crumbs, milk, egg, minced onion, Worcestershire sauce, and marjoram. Season with salt and pepper. Mix well. Shape mixture into 2-inch balls.

In a large skillet melt butter over medium-high heat. Add meatballs; brown on all sides. Spoon off any drippings. Pour in wine. Reduce heat to medium-low. Cook, covered, 25 minutes. Stir in cheese; cook another 10 minutes. 6 servings.

BERNER PLATTE

The *Berner Platte*, named for the attractive Swiss capital of Bern, is a national specialty. Once it was a typical farmer's dish, eaten in the home and served at wedding or christening feasts. Now it's prepared for parties to be enjoyed by hearty diners. Made of an assortment of meats, sausages, and vegetables, it's always fun to order as the ingredients are apt to be quite interesting, sometimes including pigs' hocks, ears, and tongue. This is one version of the dish.

2 pounds sauerkraut
2 tablespoons bacon or pork fat
2 medium yellow onions, peeled and chopped
8 peppercorns
10 juniper berries
2½ cups dry white wine
½ pound bacon in one piece
6 smoked pork chops
1 pound pork sausage links, cooked and drained
6 bratwurst or knockwurst, braised and drained
6 thick slices cooked ham
6 medium potatoes, boiled, drained and peeled, kept hot
3 cups cooked and drained hot green beans
3 tablespoons unsalted butter
1 garlic clove, minced
Salt, freshly ground pepper

Rinse sauerkraut; drain well to remove all liquid. In a pot heat the fat over medium-high heat. Add onions; sauté until translucent, about 5 minutes. Add sauerkraut; sauté, mixing with a fork, for 5 minutes. Add peppercorns, juniper berries, wine, and bacon. Reduce heat to medium-low. Add pork chops, sausage, bratwurst or knockwurst, and ham. Continue cooking until ingredients are cooked, about 30 minutes. Remove and discard the peppercorns and juniper berries.

To serve, spoon sauerkraut onto a platter. Surround with the meats. Put hot potatoes in a medium bowl; combine hot green beans, butter and garlic, seasoned with salt and pepper, in another bowl. Serve as accompaniments. 6 to 8 servings.

ÉMINCÉ DE VEAU

The Swiss are devotees of veal that cooks prepare in inviting dishes made with small strips of the tender meat. One of the specialties named *émincé* is now an international favorite made with veal strips sautéed in butter and cooked in a white wine-cream sauce. The name derives from the French *émincer*, meaning to cut into slices. Very often *émincé* also includes mushrooms. It is served traditionally with *rösti*. This is a recipe for a version of the dish I enjoyed in St. Gallen.

2 pounds very thin veal cutlets
About 6 tablespoons unsalted butter
2 tablespoons minced shallots or scallions
1 cup dry white wine
1¼ cups heavy cream
Salt, freshly ground pepper

Trim any fat from cutlets and discard it. Cut veal into slivers about ¼ inch wide and 2½ inches long.

In a large skillet melt 3 tablespoons butter over medium-high heat. Add half the veal slivers. Sauté, mixing about with a fork, until tender, about 2 minutes. Remove to a plate; keep warm. Add 3 more tablespoons butter to the skillet and heat. Add remaining veal slices; cook in the same way. Remove to a platter. Add shallots or scallions to the drippings and include more butter, if needed. Sauté for 1 minute. Pour in wine. Bring to a boil. Cook over high heat to reduce almost to half. Add cream. Reduce heat to medium-low. Cook, stirring, for 1 minute. Add veal and any juices. Leave on the stove long enough to heat through. Season with salt and pepper. 4 to 6 servings.

FONDUE BOURGUIGNONNE

Another delightful fondue that has become an international favorite is this one of beef. It differs, however, from the famous cheese fondue in that the meat is cooked in oil and dipped in sauces afterward. There is great appeal to this type of cookery, as all the ingredients can be prepared beforehand, and the beef is cooked at the table. Necessary for the cooking is a fondue pot or similar utensil, long-handled forks, dinner plates, and small bowls for the sauces. Traditional accompaniments for the fondue are deep-fried, thinly sliced potatoes or baked potatoes and a green salad. The Swiss enjoy a dry red wine with the fondue. Although any good beef may be used, a tender cut such as sirloin is preferable. A few sauce recipes are included below but prepared sauces may be used, if desired. These might include tartar or chili sauce or Russian dressing.

3 pounds boneless beef tenderloin, sirloin, or other beef
Peanut oil
Assorted Sauces

Cut off any fat from the beef and discard it. Cut beef into 1-inch cubes. Pile on a platter or wooden board. When it is time to cook the meat have the table set with an empty plate, long-handled fork, dinner fork (and other necessary implements if other foods are included) for each person.

Put enough oil to be 1½ to 2 inches deep into the fondue pot and heat it. Each person spears a cube of meat with a long-handled fork and cooks it in the hot oil to the desired degree of doneness. The meat is then taken from the long-handled fork onto the plate and eaten with a dinner fork after dipping in one or more sauces. Continue the cooking until all the meat is used. 4 servings.

SAUCES

MUSTARD SAUCE

Combine 1 cup of sour cream, 2 tablespoons prepared mustard, and 2 teaspoons prepared horseradish.

TARTAR SAUCE

Combine 1 cup of mayonnaise, ¼ cup chopped sweet pickle, 3 tablespoons chopped scallions, 1 tablespoon minced fresh parsley, and 1 teaspoon prepared mustard. Season with salt and pepper.

RUSSIAN DRESSING

Combine 1 cup mayonnaise, ½ cup chili sauce, and 3 table-spoons pickle relish. Season with salt and pepper.

RÖSTI

A national Swiss potato dish called *rösti* or *röesti* is made of cold cooked potatoes that are first grated and then sautéed in butter so that they form a cake. In some versions grated cheese, onion, or ham is added to the potatoes.

2 pounds (6 medium) potatoes, washed
Salt
About 4 tablespoons unsalted butter

In a medium saucepan put the potatoes in their skins in a little salted boiling water over medium-high heat. Cook until just tender, about 20 minutes. Drain; peel and cool. Refrigerate to chill. Grate coarsely.

In a medium skillet (about 10 inches) melt 4 tablespoons butter over medium-high heat. Add grated potatoes. Flatten with a spatula into a thin cake. Fry, uncovered, until a golden crust forms on the bottom, about 7 minutes. Shake the pan occasionally so it does not stick. Loosen around the edges. Put a plate over the top; invert onto the plate. Add more butter and then return the potato cake to the pan. Cook until golden brown on the other side. Slide the potato cake onto a warm plate. 6 servings.

BERN STUFFED ONIONS

Switzerland's federal capital city of Bern, a handsome preserved medieval city, is the only place in the world that sets aside a special day to honor the humble onion. Annually, on the fourth Monday of November, thousands of Swiss and foreign celebrants gather at a colorful Onion Market (*Zwiebele Marit*) to enjoy an unusual autumn harvest holiday enlivened with good eating and merrymaking.

The celebration dates back to May 14, 1405, when a devastating fire destroyed most of the city and help from neighboring Fribourg enabled the citizens to survive and recover. As special thanks, the Bern city council officially granted the farmers of Fribourg a privilege "for all time" to hold a market one day each year.

In the early days the market featured a variety of vegetables but over the years onions, the region's most important crop, became the primary attraction. Onions always have been a national favorite. In fact, at one time the Swiss even wore onions in necklaces as charms against the plague and illness. Here is a recipe for one of the many Swiss onion specialties.

4 medium yellow onions
Salt
½ cup soft bread crumbs
2 tablespoons milk
1 small egg, beaten
¼ cup chopped fresh parsley
Freshly ground pepper
4 teaspoons fine dry bread crumbs
4 teaspoons grated Emmental or Gruyère
1 to 2 teaspoons unsalted butter
½ cup beef bouillon

Preheat oven to 375 degrees.

Peel onions; cut a slice from the top of each one. In a large saucepan parboil onions in salted boiling water over medium-high heat for 15 minutes. With a slotted spoon remove and cool onions. Take out the centers leaving a shell about 2 rings thick. Be careful not to break the outer shell.

In a medium bowl combine soft bread crumbs and milk. Stir in beaten egg and parsley. Season with pepper. Spoon mixture into onions, dividing evenly. Sprinkle tops with dry bread crumbs and cheese. Dot with butter. Arrange in a shallow baking dish. Add bouillon. Bake, uncovered, until onions are tender, about 30 minutes, basting with juices once or twice during the cooking. 4 servings.

Note: Use onion centers for another dish or sauté in butter and serve separately.

CHANTERELLES WITH SOUR CREAM SAUCE

The Swiss are devotees of flavorful wild mushrooms, especially the chanterelle which is cup-shaped with a frilly edge and shallow gills and of a pale or dark egg yolk color. It is so distinctive that it cannot be confused with any other. In America the mushrooms are sold in cans and dried form.

1 can (4 ounces) chanterelles
5 to 6 tablespoons unsalted butter
2 slices white bread, halved and crusts removed
1 tablespoon chopped shallots or scallions
⅛ teaspoon freshly grated nutmeg
Salt, freshly ground pepper
2 tablespoons all-purpose flour
½ cup sour cream
2 tablespoons grated Swiss cheese

Preheat oven to 375 degrees.

Drain and slice chanterelles. In a medium skillet melt 4 tablespoons butter over medium-high heat. Add bread halves; sauté on both sides until golden. Remove to a buttered shallow baking dish. Add remaining 1 to 2 tablespoons butter to the skillet. Add shallots or scallions; sauté 2 minutes. Add sliced chanterelles. Sauté 4 minutes. With a slotted spoon remove from the skillet and spread over the sautéed bread. Sprinkle with nutmeg, salt, and pepper. Stir flour into the pan drippings. Whisk to blend well. Add sour cream; mix well. Heat, stirring constantly, until sauce is thickened. Pour over chanterelles, spreading evenly. Sprinkle with the cheese. Put in oven until the cheese is melted, about 7 minutes. 2 servings.

GREEN SALAD WITH CHEESE

The best cheese for this salad is flavorful Emmental. Serve the salad as a first course or accompaniment for roast meat or steaks.

 1 medium head chicory
 1 small head leafy lettuce
 ½ pound Emmental cheese, cut into cubes or slivers
 2 tablespoons drained capers
 ½ cup sour cream
 2 tablespoons wine vinegar
 1 to 2 teaspoons sharp prepared mustard
 1 teaspoon prepared horseradish
 Salt, freshly ground pepper

Wash and dry chicory and lettuce; tear into bite-size pieces; refrigerate. When ready to serve, put greens in a salad bowl. Add cheese and capers; toss lightly. In a small dish combine the sour cream, vinegar, mustard, and horseradish. Season with salt and pepper. Spoon over the salad; toss. 4 to 6 servings.

APPENZELL APPLE-CHEESE SALAD

Appenzell is the name of both a canton and town in northeastern Switzerland that has maintained many ancient customs. The local people are often dressed in their colorful folk costumes and buildings are gaily painted on the outside with decorative designs. A renovated Museum Appenzell features local handicrafts and artifacts. Among the culinary specialties are Appenzeller cheese, crisp golden fritters made in fancy patterns, spice honey cakes (*biberli*), as well as Appenzeller bitters (a sweet aperitif), and an *eau-de-vie* made of blended herbs. Some of the region's salads include apples and cheese. This is one of them.

4 unpeeled, cored red apples, diced
2 tablespoons fresh lemon juice
1 cup diced celery
1 cup shredded Appenzeller or Gruyère cheese
About 1 cup mayonnaise
1 tablespoon sharp prepared mustard
Salt, freshly ground pepper
Lettuce leaves, washed and dried
½ cup chopped walnuts

Put diced apples in a bowl or serving dish. Sprinkle with lemon juice. Add celery and cheese. In a small dish combine the mayonnaise and mustard. Season with salt and pepper. Add to apple mixture. Refrigerate, covered, up to 3 hours, to blend flavors. Serve in a mound on a plate or in lettuce "cups" sprinkled with nuts. 4 servings.

KOHLRABI SALAD

Kohlrabi, or cabbage turnip, is a purplish-white vegetable grown primarily for its swollen root, which has a pleasing, nutty flavor. It can be prepared in any of the ways that are suitable for turnips. When cooked and cold, it may be served with an oil-vinegar dressing or mayonnaise. Greatly treasured in central and northern Europe, the vegetable goes well with pork and game.

4 medium kohlrabi
Salt
½ cup sliced radishes
⅓ cup mayonnaise
2 tablespoons cider vinegar
½ teaspoon dry mustard
1 teaspoon sugar
Salt, freshly ground pepper
Crisp lettuce leaves, washed and dried
½ cup grated scraped carrots

Cut off tops and pare thick kohlrabi stems. Cut into slices. In a medium saucepan cook, covered, in a little salted boiling water over medium-high heat until tender, about 15 minutes. Drain and cool. In a serving dish or bowl combine the cooked kohlrabi slices and radishes. In a small dish combine the mayonnaise, vinegar, mustard, and sugar. Season with salt and pepper. Add to vegetables. Mix well. Refrigerate, covered, up to 6 hours to blend flavors. Serve on lettuce leaves, garnished with shredded carrots. 4 to 6 servings.

APPLE CAKE

This apple-topped cake, or *kuchen,* is a favorite Swiss dessert.

½ cup (1 stick) unsalted butter, softened
¾ cup plus 2 tablespoons sugar
3 large eggs
1¾ cups sifted all-purpose flour
½ teaspoon salt
2 teaspoons baking powder
1 tablespoon grated lemon rind
2 medium tart apples, peeled and cored
Strawberry jam

Preheat oven to 350 degrees. Butter a 9-inch springform cake pan.

In a large bowl cream the butter and ¾ cup sugar. Add eggs, one at a time. Beat until light and fluffy. Sift flour, salt, and baking powder; add with lemon rind to creamed ingredients. Mix well. Turn into prepared cake pan, spreading evenly.

Cut each apple into 4 wedges; then cut from rounded sides into thin slices. Arrange attractively over the batter; sprinkle with 2 tablespoons sugar. Bake until tester inserted into center of the cake comes out clean, about 1 hour. Brush apples with jam. Cool on a rack. To serve, cut into wedges. 12 servings.

ST. GALLEN STRAWBERRY TORTE

Founded in 612 A.D. by the Irish monk Gallus, the cultural town of St. Gallen in the foothills of the northeastern Alps, is famous for its lace and embroidery, cathedral, textile museum, and library with rare manuscripts. One of its noted specialties is St. Gallen bratwurst. Others are an almond bar and almond-chocolate torte. In the town are several historic hotels and restaurants serving local sausages, cheese and pasta dishes, and fruit tortes. The recipe for this modern version of a torte was given to me by a Swiss friend.

> ½ cup (1 stick) unsalted butter, softened
> 1½ cups plus 3 tablespoons sugar
> 4 eggs, separated
> 2 cups sifted cake flour
> 1 teaspoon baking powder
> ¼ cup milk
> 1 teaspoon vanilla
> ½ cup chopped almonds
> 1 cup heavy cream
> 1 package (1 pound) frozen sliced strawberries, thawed
> and drained

Preheat oven to 350 degrees. Line two 9-inch layer-cake pans with wax paper.

In a large bowl cream butter and ½ cup sugar until light and fluffy. Add egg yolks; beat well. Sift cake flour and baking powder, adding alternately with milk, to the creamed mixture. Mix well. Turn batter into prepared pans, spreading evenly.

In a large bowl beat egg whites until stiff. Add 1 cup sugar and vanilla. Beat again. Spoon evenly over the batter. Sprinkle with almonds. Bake until tester inserted into center comes out clean, about 25 minutes. Cool in pans, then remove the pans.

In a large bowl whip the cream with 3 tablespoons sugar until stiff. Add berries. Spoon some of the mixture over one meringue layer. Top with the other; cover the top and sides with the cream-berry mixture. Refrigerate until ready to serve. 4 servings.

SWISS CHOCOLATE

To many people, Switzerland means chocolate. The Swiss are truly a nation of chocolate lovers. They eat and drink more of it than any other nation and they make the most seductive candies. Hotels offer hot cocoa or chocolate for breakfast and the Swiss have morning breaks for these beverages in their offices and factories. Mountaineers carry chocolate with them and children eat it with bread for snacks. Attractive, aromatic chocolate shops have handsome displays of the famous Tobler, Lindt, Villars, and Nestle solid bars, as well as exquisitely printed boxes of the candy, chocolate sculptures, coins, truffles, and all kinds of chocolates filled with fruits, creams, and liqueurs.

A love affair with chocolate began in Switzerland after the introduction of it from the New World to Europe where it became a fashionable beverage. No one is certain how and when solid chocolate was created. Until the nineteenth century, however, it was dry, coarse, and grainy in texture, as well as rare and expensive. Two great developments in the production and improvement of the food took place in Switzerland, and consequently the Swiss became masters in the art of making chocolate. About 1875 Henri Nestlé, a chemist in Vevey, worked with Daniel Peter, a chocolatier, to mix sweetened condensed milk with chocolate liquor. Thus milk chocolate was born. In 1879 another Swiss chocolatier, Rodolphe Lindt, developed the chocolate-kneading technique known as conching, which produces a smooth-textured solid eating chocolate. Later, in 1908, Theodore Tobler, also a Swiss, created Toblerone, a milk chocolate bar with almonds and honey.

Besides eating chocolate, the Swiss cook with it, and over the years, have created an array of delectable cakes, pies, cookies, pastries, desserts, sauces, confections, and drinks. One of their favorite beverages is hot chocolate, enjoyed throughout the day and night, especially for breakfast and in mid-afternoon. It's the perfect cold weather beverage. Here is a basic recipe for it.

2 squares (2 ounces) unsweetened chocolate
½ cup sugar
Dash salt
⅓ cup hot water
2 cups milk
Whipped cream

In the top of a double boiler over simmering water melt the chocolate. Add the sugar, salt, and hot water; stir well. Cook 1 or 2 minutes. Gradually add milk and heat. Remove from the heat. Whisk until frothy. Pour into individual mugs. Serve topped with whipped cream. 4 servings.

SWISS WINES

Swiss wine? Yes. The Swiss have been making wines for hundreds of years, dating back to the time of the Romans. It is believed that vine plants were introduced to Switzerland by a Swiss mercenary Hellico returning from Rome. But it's possible that there were vineyards in Switzerland before the Roman times, especially near the Lakes of Neuchâtel, Geneva, and Zurich. Later, monks of different orders, coming primarily from France, encouraged wine growing, especially around the twelfth century. Attached to some Swiss wines are centuries-old legends that are significant to the celebrations of the autumn wine harvests.

Although they are not well known abroad, and wine is not a major industry, Switzerland produces many wonderful wines from vineyards along its sunny lake shores, and even at terraces at over 3,600 feet near the Matterhorn. They are as varied as the climates and soils in which they flourish. For the most part, however, the viniculture areas follow the four national languages: Swiss-German and Romansch in the East, French in the West, and Italian in the South. The vines and wines, as well as the villages and people, reflect the distinctive characters and flavors of each region.

All wine names in Switzerland are geographic and carry the name of a specific region, canton, local town, or parish. More than half of all Swiss wine, however, is white, made from the Chasselas grape that produces a fresh, lively wine. It has a natural sparkle or crispness that distinguishes it from the wines of nearby vineyards in other countries.

In the east, the Thurgau, Schaffhausen, and Lake Constance areas, plus the alpine valley of the Rhine, the red, white, and rosé wines are light and subtle.

The Swiss like to tell visitors to their country that the reason their wines are not popular in other lands is that they are so good that they like to drink them all. Since many of the best Swiss wines never even leave their village, the preferable way to enjoy their wonderfully diverse tastes is right where they are made. It's always a pleasure to enjoy a good local wine with delicious food.

Being light, the Swiss wines are adaptable. While their principal use is for the table, they may also be drunk as an aperitif or used in cooking to enhance the flavor of a dish. They go equally well with a fish course, the main dish, with cheese, or with dessert. They are perfect with the well-known Swiss specialty, fondue. All Swiss wines, either white or red, adapt themselves perfectly to cheese.

Annual Swiss wine festivals, held in September and October in several regions, are lively events and well worth looking for. Specific information about them can be obtained from local tourist offices.

Basel, Switzerland.

SWISS SPIRITS

For hundreds of years Switzerland has been a noted producer of spirits distilled from fruit and known as fruit brandies or *eaux de vie*. The country's most famous and treasured is kirsch, a fragrant, crystal-clear potent drink with an exquisite flavor that is made from cherries. The Swiss enjoy it at the end of a meal, often with or in black coffee. It goes well with fruit, and is sprinkled over desserts or ice cream. It also adds distinction to sweet sauces.

Equally prized for its delicate bouquet is pear brandy, a colorless distillate of pears that looks like kirsch but has the unusual pronounced aroma and flavor of the pear. Sometimes this has a fruit in the bottle. One notable example is Williams Pear Brandy that has a pear in the bottom of the bottle. Raspberry brandy is the most delicate of the pure fruit distillations.

The Swiss also are devotees of strong herb-flavored liqueurs, enjoyed as aperitifs or after a meal. It is believed that they stimulate the appetite and are good for the health and digestion. Commonly made from alpine herbs and flowers, they include Enzian, distilled from the roots of the wild gentian; and Appenzeller Alpenbitter, made from extracts of more than fifty alpine plants. It is sweet as well as bitter.

LIECHTENSTEIN

An Alpine Storybook Principality

Government Building in Vaduz.

There's something about the charming country called Liechtenstein along the eastern bank of the Rhine River and nestled in the Alps that makes me think of it as a fairy tale. But it is not. For there's an actual storybook land with a handsome prince and towering majestic castle where he and his family live in an alpine world of spectacular scenery with quaint villages, orchards, vineyards, and luxuriant meadows. And in this pastoral paradise there are practically no taxes, no poverty, no unemployment, no army, and crime is virtually unknown.

A great place for travelers, sports enthusiasts, historians, and gourmets, the tiny Principality of Liechtenstein in the heart of Europe has a host of diverse attractions. It's where I found openhearted people, unique postage stamps, art museums, cozy inns, and inviting dining places serving genuine food. One of the traditions the citizens are especially proud of is making wine.

Covering only 62 square miles, Liechtenstein is the fourth smallest state in Europe, situated between Austria and Switzerland with eleven communities and just over 30,000 residents. Its scenery is breathtaking, and the way of life a page from yesteryear.

It was a place I had to see. And, like many visitors, I went there while on the way to somewhere else. After leaving Switzerland and, en route to Germany, we were still following the Rhine which flows along the length of the Principality from south to north. Then, once across a narrow wooden bridge over the river, I could see the turreted castle of Liechtenstein, and felt an air of enchantment. Traveling the single main road that extends from border to border, the visitor is soon captivated by the tranquil and friendly atmosphere of the country.

As we soon discovered, this amazing nation has a lot of charm and many cheerful citizens who greet visitors with a friendly *Grüss Gott* or "Greetings." No throwback to another age, the Principality is a prosperous and remarkable state with a high standard of living. It's also one of the last oases on the continent where life is enjoyed at a leisurely and graceful pace. Few airplanes buzz overhead, since there is no airport. (The nearest is in Zurich.) Cyclists and pedestrians are prevalent and the post bus network is well developed. The railway only passes through a part of the nation.

On entering Liechtenstein from Switzerland, it is difficult at first to realize that you've crossed an international border. None of the customary formalities and currency declarations are required, and the scenery of snow-capped Alps and meadows looks much the same. But while the Principality shares in the alpine beauty, it treasures a character all its own. Although the population is largely German in origin and speech, the country maintains its closest ties with Switzerland which represents the Principality abroad. The Swiss franc is the legal currency. All travel documents valid for Switzerland are also valid for Liechtenstein.

Colonized by Celts and Rhaetians and settled by the Romans, the Principality, however, was formed after Prince Johann Adam of Liechtenstein bought the domain of Schellenberg (now the Unterland or north) in 1699, and the county of Vaduz (now the Oberland or south) in 1712. Today the country is a constitutional monarchy with Prince Hans-Adam II as head of state.

During the past four decades the country has experienced great economic and cultural development. From being an agrarian state, Liechtenstein has developed into being one of the world's most industrialized countries. But it has not abandoned agriculture entirely. Grain and vegetables are still grown, and many orchards and vineyards are in operation. Each autumn, the ringing bells announce the beginning of the grape harvest, something in which Liechtensteiners of all ages participate.

A postage-stamp size country in itself, Liechtenstein has long attracted philatelists who come to purchase its limited-edition stamps and visit displays of rare and artistic philatelic creations at the Postage Stamp Museum in Vaduz ("Sweet Valley"), the capital. Regardless of their ultimate destination, most visitors to the country pause in Vaduz, once a farming village known for its outstanding wine, and now the seat of government. Strolling along the main street, the *städtle*, or sitting at a sidewalk café, one soon adopts the infectious spirit of friendliness of the local populace. Small shops and boutiques specialize in local handicraft products, jewelry, and stamps. Here also is the National Museum (presently closed) in a former tavern and customs house, and the National Art Collection with a small portion of the prince's collection, one of the most valuable in the world. Vaduz Castle, residence of the prince and his family, stands on a high mountain terrace, watching over the town. It is not open to the public.

My particular desire, however, was to dine at the notable restaurant in the Hotel Real, a family-run landmark on the main square renown for its fine cuisine. While there is nothing pretentious about the décor, one appreciates the old-world ambiance and geniality of the clientele. Named for its founder and former chef, Felix Real, it is now run by his son, Martin. Much of the country's gastronomic reputation can be attributed to Felix and his brother Emil, also a chef who has had a long association with the luxurious Park-Hotel Sonnenhof, a hillside retreat set in handsome gardens above Vaduz, with a spectacular view of the valleys and mountains beyond.

Menus at the Real feature foods in season with an emphasis on game, poultry, and fish, as well as inviting dishes reflecting the Principality's location between Switzerland and Austria, not far from Italy. Much of the fare also has a light French touch. Our luncheon, served with wines from the family's vineyards, was an extraordinary repast, one of the most memorable of my Rhine meals.

Another rewarding dining place in Vaduz is the Torkel, located in the prince's vineyards and named after the giant seventeenth-century wine press (Torkel), still on the premises. Here one dines on excellent dishes made with local recipes as well as European specialties. The Lowen, noted for its seasonal highlights and regional dishes, is the country's oldest inn, dating back to 1380. Set in scenic vineyards with a view of the castle, it has an attractive garden restaurant.

Many mountainside inns, village hotels, and comfortable restaurants in Liechtenstein offer pleasant lodgings, warm hospitality, and superb local fare. Dining in the Principality is a rewarding experience that embraces international cuisine as well as home-style cooking, and, as a local chef states, often incorporates new, imaginative approaches to both. The dishes go especially well with the variety of local wines.

Among the Principality's national dishes are: *sauerkas*, a piquant local cheese; hearty vegetable-meat soups; *hafalääb*, a one-dish meal made of wheat flour and cornmeal dumplings, simmered with smoked bacon or ham in broth; schnitzels, smoked pork and sauerkraut stews; venison; as well as cheese, meat, and vegetable fondues. Good desserts vary from fruit-filled pancakes to rich pastries and cakes.

Liechtenstein cookery reflects not only devotion to national tradition but also creative assimilation and adaptation of foreign influences. The following selection of traditional and representative recipes offers an introduction to a captivating cuisine that deserves to be better known.

Traditional costume procession.

TRIESEN SAUERKRAUT-HAM APPETIZERS

Located on the Rhine River at the foot of the Liechtenstein Alps, the village of Triesen, once inhabited by Roman nobility, has some notable chapels and shrines. Local restaurants serve regional home-style dishes including those made with sauerkraut and ham. Serve this appetizer before an informal winter meal.

2 tablespoons unsalted butter
1 medium yellow onion, peeled and minced
2 cups ground or minced cooked ham
1 tablespoon Dijon-style mustard
3 tablespoons minced fresh parsley
2 cups sauerkraut, drained and finely chopped
About ⅔ cup all-purpose flour
½ cup beef bouillon
Freshly ground pepper
2 eggs, beaten
About ½ cup fine dry bread crumbs
Fat or oil for frying

In a medium saucepan melt butter over medium-high heat. Add minced onion; sauté until translucent, about 3 minutes. Add ham; cook, stirring, 5 minutes. Add mustard, parsley, sauerkraut, ½ cup flour, and bouillon. Season with pepper. Mix well. Reduce heat to medium-low. Cook, stirring frequently, for 10 minutes. Turn mixture onto a platter to cool. Shape into 1-inch balls. Refrigerate, covered with plastic wrap, for 1 hour, up to 6. Before cooking, roll the balls in remaining 3 tablespoons flour; dip into beaten eggs; and roll in bread crumbs. Fry in deep hot fat or oil (370 degrees) until golden brown. Drain on paper towels. Serve hot as appetizers. Makes about 5 dozen.

ASPARAGUS CANAPES

In Liechtenstein one of the most treasured foods is tender, plump, pearl-white asparagus, grown underground and carefully cut by hand each spring. Many restaurants, including the Real in Vaduz, honor this luxurious vegetable with special menus and festivals. Here's an easy-to-prepare appetizer that can be made with white or green asparagus.

Butter thin slices of rye bread or pumpernickel, cut into 1 × 3-inch rectangles. Place a cooked fresh asparagus spear on each one. Sprinkle with a little lemon juice, fresh or dried thyme, seasoned with salt and pepper. Pipe or spoon mayonnaise along the top and around the edges. Serve at once or refrigerate, covered with plastic wrap, until ready to serve.

SCHAAN WATERCRESS SOUP

Schaan, a village of gardens and flower-decked homes just north of Vaduz, is one of the country's oldest settlements. The Romans, recognizing its perfect location along the Rhine, built a fort here. Parts of it have been excavated and can be seen around the twelfth century Romanesque church of St. Peter. A local restaurant named St. Peter serves a variety of Tyrolean dumplings and good soups.

A tangy aromatic herb, watercress belongs to the mustard family and is rich in calcium and vitamin C. Central Europeans truly appreciate watercress, which they use in sandwiches, salads, purées, and in soups. It is welcomed with great fanfare in the spring, and there is even an old belief that watercress sharpens the memory. Watercress should be handled with care, washed gently in cold water, drained well, and used as soon as possible. This soup is a good first course for a luncheon or dinner.

2 bunches fresh watercress
1 cup boiling salted water
4 tablespoons (½ stick) unsalted butter
1 small yellow onion, peeled and minced
4 tablespoons all-purpose flour
Salt, freshly ground pepper
3 cups light cream

Wash watercress; remove stems and bruised leaves. In a medium saucepan combine watercress and water over medium-high heat. Cook, covered, for 10 minutes. Purée in a food processor or press through a sieve.

In a large saucepan melt butter over medium-high heat. Add minced onion; sauté until translucent, about 3 minutes. Stir in flour. Season with salt and pepper. Cook 1 minute. Reduce heat to medium-low. Gradually add cream. Cook, stirring, until thickened and smooth. Stir in puréed watercress and liquid. Leave on stove long enough to heat through, about 5 minutes. 4 to 6 servings.

BEEF BOUILLON WITH LIVER DUMPLINGS

In Liechtenstein one of the typical dishes is a clear soup made with a rich broth that includes small dumplings or pastries. Here are recipes for liver dumplings and bread dumplings as well as the broth.

1 pound beef chuck, cut into cubes
1 small carrot, scraped
1 small yellow onion, peeled and chopped
4 sprigs parsley
1 leek, white part only, cleaned and sliced
2 tablespoons chopped celery leaves
6 cups water
Salt, freshly ground pepper

In a pot combine beef cubes, carrot, chopped onion, parsley, leek, celery leaves, and water over medium-high heat. Season with salt and pepper. Bring to a boil. Remove any scum from the top. Reduce heat to medium-low. Cook, covered, 1½ hours. Skim again. Strain bouillon. Correct seasoning. Reheat bouillon over medium-high heat. Drop in Liver Dumplings (recipe below). Cook, covered, until dumplings rise to the surface, about 10 minutes. Spoon dumplings into large soup bowls. Spoon broth over them. 6 servings.

LIVER DUMPLINGS

½ pound beef liver, ground or minced
2 tablespoons unsalted butter, softened
1 small garlic clove, crushed
½ teaspoon grated lemon rind
⅛ teaspoon dried marjoram
⅛ teaspoon freshly grated nutmeg
Salt, freshly ground pepper
2 eggs, beaten
About 1¼ cups fine dry bread crumbs

In a large bowl or food processor container, combine the liver, butter, garlic, lemon rind, marjoram, and nutmeg. Season with salt and pepper. Mix or purée the ingredients. Turn mixture into a large bowl. Add eggs; mix well. Stir in enough bread crumbs to make a stiff mixture. Form into tiny balls. Leave at room temperature for 1 hour. If not stiff enough, add more bread crumbs. Add to bouillon as directed above.

BREAD DUMPLINGS

Tiny German-inspired dumplings or noodles, called *knöpfli* or *spätzli*, are made in many varieties. Some may include cheese, ham, or bacon. They are served in soups, as accompaniments, or a light main dish with gravy or a favorite sauce.

2½ cups all-purpose flour
½ teaspoon salt
2 eggs, lightly beaten
Boiling salted water

Into a large bowl sift the flour and salt. Make a well in the center. Add eggs and ½ cup water. Beat, adding more water as necessary, to make a stiff dough. Beat with a wooden spoon until soft and light. Let stand 30 minutes. Turn out on a dampened wooden board or flat surface. Roll out to a ⅛-inch thickness. With a sharp knife, cut off small strips or slivers.

In a saucepan of boiling salted water over medium-high heat, drop several strips or slivers at a time. Cook until they rise to the top, 3 to 5 minutes. With a slotted spoon, remove from the water; drain. Makes about 4 cups.

CORNMEAL PUDDING

A national dish called *rebl* or *ribel*, made with cornmeal or a mixture of half cornmeal and half semolina, was once a main source of nourishment, prepared in various forms for morning and evening meals in Liechtenstein. As a thick mush it is eaten by itself, usually with gravy or a sauce, vegetables or meats. A traditional accompaniment is elderberry purée. Here are two recipes for the dish.

In a large saucepan bring 2½ cups salted water to a boil over medium-high heat. Slowly add 1 cup yellow cornmeal; stirring vigorously with a wooden spoon while adding, until mixture is thick and smooth. The water should continue to boil. Reduce heat to medium-low. Continue to cook, covered, until meal takes shape of pan, about 12 minutes. Run a knife around its edges; invert onto a plate. Serve hot, plain, with melted butter, grated cheese, or with gravy. 4 servings.

Fried: Cool cooked cornmeal (recipe above); cut into slices. Dip each slice in beaten egg. Sprinkle generously on each side with grated yellow cheese. In a medium skillet fry in hot melted butter over medium-high heat on both sides until golden. Serve with sour cream or berry purée.

TRIESENBERG CHEESE-NOODLE CASSEROLE

In the village of Triesenberg, 3,000 feet high in the Liechtenstein Alps, one can enjoy spectacular views of the Rhine Valley. The unique history of this Walser community, founded by settlers who came from Valais, Switzerland, in the thirteen century, is documented in the folklore museum and by the village's Valaisan-style houses.

Favorite local specialties include noodle or pasta dishes flavored with sour cream, cheese, and bacon. Serve this one as an accompaniment to roast pork, chicken, or beef.

¼ pound sliced bacon
½ cup chopped onions
1 package (8 ounces) wide noodles, cooked and drained
1½ cups cottage cheese
1 cup sour cream, at room temperature
Salt, freshly ground pepper
2 tablespoons chopped fresh dill or parsley

Preheat oven to 350 degrees. Butter a 1½-quart round baking dish.

In a medium skillet fry the bacon over medium-high heat until crisp. With a slotted spoon remove and drain. Add onions to bacon drippings. Sauté until translucent, about 4 minutes. Remove from heat.

In a large bowl combine the cooked onions and drippings, cooked noodles, cottage cheese, and sour cream. Season with salt and pepper. Spoon into prepared baking dish. Arrange bacon slices over the top. Sprinkle with dill or parsley. Bake until ingredients are firm and light golden, about 30 minutes. 4 servings.

ESCHEN BAKED TROUT

Eschen, the main community of the northern lowland that incorporates the village of Nendeln, has nearby prehistoric settlement sights and peaceful historical paths. One of the region's culinary specialties is fresh trout from alpine streams.

6 slices thin bacon
6 fresh or thawed quick-frozen trout
Salt, freshly ground pepper
¼ cup chopped fresh parsley
¼ cup chopped chives
2 tablespoons all-purpose flour
3 tablespoons unsalted butter, softened
½ cup fine cracker or bread crumbs

Preheat oven to 400 degrees.

Arrange 3 slices bacon in a shallow baking dish. Wash trout; wipe dry. Sprinkle with salt and pepper. Combine parsley and chives; sprinkle over the bacon. Place trout on top. In a small dish blend the flour and butter. Spread on the trout. Sprinkle with crumbs.

Arrange 3 remaining slices of bacon over the trout. Bake, uncovered, until fish flakes but is still moist, about 15 minutes. Serve at once. 6 servings.

PORK TOKANY

Central Europeans are fond of hearty stews. Tokany is a paprika-flavored pork or beef stew for which the meat is cut into strips. It also includes mushrooms, vegetables, and sour cream. This is one good version of the stew.

3 tablespoons lard or vegetable oil
2 pounds lean boneless pork, cut into 3-by-1-inch strips
Salt, freshly ground pepper
1 tablespoon paprika
1 large yellow onion, peeled and chopped
1 large carrot, scraped and thinly sliced
1 large green pepper, cleaned and sliced
2 large red tomatoes, peeled and chopped
2 cups sliced mushrooms
1 tablespoon all-purpose flour
1 cup sour cream, at room temperature

In a large saucepan heat the lard or oil over medium-high heat. Add pork strips and brown. Season with salt and pepper. Add paprika and chopped onion; sauté until translucent, about 5 minutes. Reduce heat to medium-low. Cook, covered, 30 minutes. Add sliced carrot, green pepper, and tomatoes. Continue cooking 20 minutes. Add mushrooms. In a small dish combine flour with a little hot sauce. Stir into stew. Add sour cream. Cook another 5 minutes. Serve at once. 4 to 6 servings.

BALZERS SPLIT PEA–SAUSAGE STEW

Balzers, Liechtenstein's southernmost village, in the Rhine Valley, is set among rolling meadows and vineyards and dominated by the towering Gutenberg Castle, perched atop a high craggy rock. One of the most interesting places to dine here is the *Gasthous* Engel, located in a historic landmark building, that serves home-style dishes including *geshnetzeltes* (thin slices of meat with gravy), *rösti* (shredded potato cake), and sausages. Here is a recipe for a hearty and nourishing sausage stew.

3 tablespoons unsalted butter
2 medium yellow onions, peeled and diced
2 medium carrots, scraped and diced
2 medium stalks celery, cleaned and sliced thinly
2 cups (1 pound) green split peas, rinsed and picked over
10 cups water
½ teaspoon dried oregano
½ teaspoon dried thyme
⅛ teaspoon paprika
Salt, freshly ground pepper
1 pound sausage links, fried and sliced thickly
2 tablespoons minced fresh parsley

In a pot melt butter over medium-high heat. Add diced onions, carrots, and celery. Sauté 5 minutes. Add peas and water; bring to a boil. Add oregano, thyme, and paprika. Season with salt and pepper. Reduce heat to medium-low. Cook, covered, until the peas are tender, about 1 hour. Add sausage slices and parsley. Heat 5 minutes. Serve with warm corn bread. 8 servings.

RUGGELL CHEESE-MUSHROOM PUDDING

Straddling the Rhine River flatlands, the northernmost village of Ruggell is in the center of a thriving farm community. This flavorful pudding is made with three of the country's favorite foods: mushrooms, cheese, and eggs.

½ pound fresh mushrooms
3 tablespoons unsalted butter
1 medium yellow onion, peeled and minced
2 tablespoons all-purpose flour
1 cup light cream or milk
1 cup grated Gruyère cheese
2 tablespoons chopped fresh parsley
Dash freshly grated nutmeg
Salt, freshly ground pepper
3 large eggs, separated
Fine dry bread crumbs

Preheat oven to 350 degrees. Butter a round 1½-quart baking dish.

Wash mushrooms to remove any dirt. Slice thinly. In a medium saucepan melt butter over medium-high heat. Add minced onion; sauté until translucent, about 5 minutes. Stir in flour. Cook, stirring, 1 minute. Add the cream or milk, cheese, parsley, and nutmeg. Season with salt and pepper. Reduce heat to medium-low. Cook, stirring, until mixture is thickened and smooth and cheese is melted.

Remove from the stove. In a small bowl whisk egg yolks. Add some of the hot sauce. Mix well. Stir into mushroom mixture. In a large bowl beat egg whites until stiff. Fold into the mixture. Turn into prepared baking dish. Sprinkle the top with bread crumbs. Set in a dish of hot water. Bake until set, about 45 minutes. 4 servings.

FRIED POTATO CAKE

This Swiss-inspired shredded, fried potato cake called *rösti*, often includes onions and cheese. In Liechtenstein one popular version, *alplerrösti*, is flavored with ham or bacon cubes, topped with a slice of Gruyère cheese, and served with a fried egg. It's a good supper dish.

2 pounds (6 medium), potatoes, washed
1 small yellow onion, peeled and minced
½ cup diced Gruyère cheese
Salt
About 5 tablespoons unsalted butter

In a large saucepan boil potatoes in a little salted boiling water over medium-high heat until just tender, about 20 minutes. Drain and cool. Refrigerate 1 hour. Peel and grate coarsely. In a medium bowl combine grated potatoes, onion, and cheese. Season with salt. In a large skillet melt 2 tablespoons butter over medium-high heat. Add potato mixture; flatten with a spatula into a thin cake. Cook until a golden crust forms on the bottom, shaking the pan occasionally so it does not stick. Loosen around the edges. Put a plate over the top; invert onto a plate. Add more butter; return potato cake to the pan. Cook until golden brown on the other side. 4 servings.

SAUERKRAUT WITH APPLES

Sauerkraut, a healthful dish rich in vitamins, phosphorous, calcium, and iron, is a favorite accompaniment for sausages, frankfurters, ham, or pork.

2 tablespoons unsalted butter or vegetable oil
1 medium yellow onion, peeled and chopped
1 pound sauerkraut, drained
½ cup beef bouillon
2 tart apples, pared, cored, and chopped
1 tablespoon brown sugar
½ teaspoon caraway seeds
Salt, freshly ground pepper

In a medium saucepan melt butter or heat the oil over medium-high heat. Add chopped onion; sauté until translucent, about 5 minutes. Add sauerkraut; sauté 2 to 3 minutes. Add bouillon, apples, sugar, and caraway seeds. Season with salt and pepper. Reduce heat to medium-low. Cook, covered, for 30 minutes. 4 servings.

VADUZ MIXED VEGETABLE SALAD

A mixed seasonal salad is one of the culinary delights I enjoyed for luncheon at the Hotel Real in Vaduz. This is an easy-to-prepare version of the salad.

1 cup drained canned corn niblets
1 can (1 pound) kidney beans, drained
1 cup chopped peeled cucumber
1 medium Bermuda onion, peeled and finely chopped
2 medium ripe tomatoes, peeled and chopped
3 tablespoons olive or vegetable oil
2 tablespoons red wine vinegar
Salt, freshly ground pepper

In a large bowl combine the corn, beans, chopped cucumber, onion, and tomatoes. Add oil and vinegar. Season with salt and pepper. Refrigerate, covered, with plastic wrap, 1 hour, up to 3, to blend flavors. 6 to 8 servings.

SPINACH SALAD

Central Europeans are devotees of fresh spinach, which they utilize in a number of interesting dishes such as this salad. Serve as a first course or a separate course after a veal or pork entrée.

1 package (10 ounces) fresh spinach
4 slices thin bacon, chopped
1 cup stale small bread cubes
1 garlic clove, crushed
3 tablespoons olive or vegetable oil
1 tablespoon wine vinegar
Salt, freshly ground pepper
2 hard-cooked eggs, shelled and finely chopped

Wash and dry spinach; remove tough stem ends and bruised leaves; tear large leaves into small pieces; refrigerate.

In a medium skillet fry the chopped bacon over medium-high heat until crisp. Remove bacon to drain on paper towels. Add bread cubes, sprinkled with crushed garlic, to bacon drippings. Sauté until golden brown, 1 to 2 minutes. Remove to drain on paper towels.

To serve, put spinach in a salad bowl. Add oil and vinegar. Season with salt and pepper. Toss. Add crisp bacon, bread cubes, and chopped eggs. Toss again. Serve at once. 4 servings.

GREEN SAUCE

This is an excellent sauce, made with green vegetables and herbs, to serve with cold fish, particularly trout or salmon.

½ cup chopped fresh spinach
½ cup chopped fresh watercress
⅓ cup chopped fresh herbs (parsley, tarragon, or chervil)
2 egg yolks or 1 whole egg
½ teaspoon dry mustard
Salt, freshly ground pepper
2 tablepoons fresh lemon juice
1 cup extra-virgin olive oil

In a medium saucepan combine spinach, watercress, and herbs with a little water over medium-low heat. Cook, covered, until greens are tender, 2 to 3 minutes. Drain well, pressing firmly with a spoon to remove all the liquid. Put through a sieve or mince finely. Cool. In a medium bowl combine the egg yolks or egg and mustard. Season with salt and pepper. Whisk or beat to mix well. Stir in 1 tablespoon lemon juice. Add ¼ cup of oil, drop by drop, beating while adding. Then add remaining tablespoon of lemon juice and ¾ cup oil alternately, beating constantly until thick. Mix in the chopped vegetables and herbs. Refrigerate, covered with plastic wrap, 1 hour, up to 4. Serve cold. Makes about 1¼ cups.

PANCAKES WITH CHOCOLATE SAUCE

This is one of the many pancake desserts that are beloved fare in the Principality. They are eaten either folded or rolled around fruit fillings. Or, they can be filled with ground nuts or served with a chocolate sauce. Each one is delightful.

2 eggs, beaten
1½ cups light cream or milk
1 tablespoon sugar
¼ teaspoon salt
1 cup sifted all-purpose flour
Unsalted butter for frying
Apricot, strawberry, or raspberry jam
1 cup chocolate sauce
2 tablespoons light rum
Finely chopped nuts (optional)

Preheat oven to 250 degrees.

In a large bowl combine beaten eggs, cream or milk, sugar, salt, and flour. Whisk until smooth. In a 7- or 8-inch skillet melt enough butter to grease it over medium-high heat. Add 3 tablespoons batter all at once. Quickly tilt pan to spread evenly. Cook until underside is golden. With a spatula turn over; cook on other side. Turn out onto a warm plate. Keep warm in oven. Continue to cook more pancakes. Spread each one with a thin layer of jam; roll or fold over. Serve at once with chocolate sauce and rum, heated together. Sprinkle with finely chopped nuts, if desired. 8 to 10 servings.

SNOWBALLS

Serve these vanilla-flavored delicate egg white balls as dessert for a company dinner.

4 eggs, separated
¾ cup sugar
⅛ teaspoon salt
2 cups milk
1 teaspoon vanilla
⅓ cup confectioners' sugar
2 tablespoons cornstarch
¼ cup water
Sliced berries (optional)

In a small bowl beat egg yolks. Add ¼ cup sugar and the salt; beat again; set aside. In a large skillet combine the milk, vanilla, and confectioners' sugar over medium-low heat. Heat to simmering. Do not boil. Meanwhile, in a large bowl beat egg whites until soft peaks form. Gradually add remaining ½ cup sugar and continue beating until mixture is thick and glossy. Drop egg white mixture by tablespoons, several at a time, into heated milk. Poach, turning once, until set, about 3 minutes. Drain on paper towels. Strain the milk into a saucepan; heat over medium-low heat to simmer. Add a little hot milk to beaten egg yolks; mix well. Return to saucepan. In a small dish combine cornstarch with water; add to milk. Cook slowly, stirring, until thickened and smooth. Spoon snowballs into a shallow bowl or serving dish. Pour custard over them. Refrigerate 1 hour, up to 3. Serve with sliced berries, if desired. 6 servings.

APPLE FROTH

This delicate dessert is easy to make with a few ingredients.

2 egg whites
2 cups chilled apple purée or applesauce
2 to 4 tablespoons sugar
1 teaspoon grated lemon rind
1 tablespoon apple brandy
Grated sweet chocolate

In a large bowl whip egg whites until stiff. Carefully fold in the apple purée or applesauce, sugar, lemon rind, and brandy. Spoon into serving dishes. Serve garnished with grated chocolate. 4 servings.

BAKED SWEET NOODLES

Central Europeans are fond of desserts made with sweetened noodles, which may be baked or fried. This is one of the best.

1 package (8 ounces) wide noodles
¼ cup (½ stick) unsalted butter, cut up
½ cup chopped walnuts or hazelnuts
About ⅓ cup sugar
3 tablespoons apricot jam
1 cup light cream
Confectioners' sugar

Preheat oven to 350 degrees. Butter a shallow 1½-quart baking dish.
Cook and drain noodles according to package instructions. While still warm, in a large bowl combine noodles with butter, nuts, sugar, and jam. Spoon into prepared baking dish. Pour cream over the ingredients. Sprinkle with confectioners' sugar. Bake until noodles are tender, about 30 minutes. 4 to 6 servings.

LIECHTENSTEIN WINES

Although Liechtenstein's vineyard area is quite small, the making of wines is an ancient tradition that is very important to the people. Nearly the entire grape harvest is made into wines and sold in the Principality. Thanks to favorable natural conditions, ideal southwest-oriented hillside locations with calcareous soil, and adequate sunshine, the grapes can come to full ripeness. Wine quality is comparable to that of nearby Swiss growing areas. Besides Pinot Gris, Chardonnay, Gewüztraminer, and Zweigelt, mainly Pinot Noir and Riesling-x-Sylvaner are cultivated and processed into wines. There are also crossbreeds such as Regent, Marechal Foch, and Leon Millet.

Wine names are usually geographic with that of the local town or parish added. Also there are sometimes local names for each varietal, and various blends available.

Today the making of wine is often in the hands of small owners in areas around the various communities. In Vaduz they adjoin the historical Löwen Inn and Rotes House, once a fortress for the bailiffs of a Swiss Benedictine monastery. Others are the princely vineyards that have names like Herawingert and Bockwingert. In Schaan there is the Bardella vineyard; in Triesen it's the Halda and St. Mamerten; while in Bendern the name is Herrgottsacker. In Balzers they include the Am runda Böchel and Schlosböchel Gutenberg.

Visitors to the Principality can enjoy wine tastings at several restaurants and inns and in the wine cellars of the prince for groups of 10 or more persons, with reservations.

AUSTRIA

Sausages, Schnitzels and Pastries

Imperial Palace, Vienna.
PHOTOGRAPHED BY WIESENHOFER.
COURTESY OF THE AUSTRIAN NATIONAL TOURIST OFFICE.

Each time I've visited the enchanting, small country of Austria, I enjoyed a memorable dining experience. Once it was a light luncheon at the foot of a spectacular snow-capped mountain featuring a mushroom dumpling. At Salzburg's famous Goldener Hirsch Hotel we enjoyed a fluffy, sweet soufflé and snowballs made of egg whites. Before the opera in Vienna, an elegant dinner featured blue trout and white asparagus. The chef's specialties at a chalet near the Yugoslav border proved to be braised veal shanks with potato dumplings. But everywhere I relished a beloved snack called *würstel*, a succulent sausage that provides pleasure as well as nourishment. Sometimes it's the simplest food that tastes best.

On a hot August afternoon, after a lengthy luncheon in Vaduz, Liechtenstein, it was a spur-of-the-moment decision to follow the Rhine River marking the border between Austria and Switzerland and to stop for a short time in one of the valley's historic towns. This would be my first visit to Vorarlberg, the pear-shaped region in Austria's extreme west and the homeland of a dear friend. She described it as an outpost, quite different from the splendor of the rest of the country.

The smallest of its nine provinces, an isolated area encompassing the plains of Lake Constance (Bodensee) and mighty alpine ranges, Vorarlberg provides exceptional skiing, dramatic landscapes, and picturesque villages. We stayed at comfortable country inns and dined on the hearty regional specialties.

Driving from one prosperous town to another, surrounded by verdant farmlands, rich meadows, and gentle hills, it would not take long to discover why the Rhine province sometimes is fondly called "the little country" or even an "independent state." Or why the distant extremity of Austria has long been closely associated with its neighbor, Switzerland. For the region's early settlers came from a nearby Swiss area; Vorarlbergers speak a dialect close to Swiss German; and the people remain self-sufficient in a great many ways. In 1918 they even declared their independence, requesting union with Switzerland. But this never took place.

One of our brief but enjoyable Vorarlberg tours began at the capital, Bregenz, then led south to the river town of Lustenau, surrounded by thousands of fruit trees, to romantic Hohenems, and on to Oberland. Here we found attractive alpine villages and an amazing variety of cherry trees that make a potent local spirit called *eau de vie*.

Since the area is a large producer of dairy products, there are several good cheeses such as Austrian Gruyère and Swiss used in many forms. Vorarlberg's favorite dishes include cheese dumplings, noodles, and puddings as well as herb-flavored soups, fish from the mountain streams and Lake Constance, and an array of smoked meat specialties. Austrian cooks have created an imaginative repertoire of dishes made with these meats and I relished many of them. But there is no equal to the humble *würstel*, a sausage that can be enjoyed any time of the day or night, preferably at a rustic stall or stand. Usually sold in pairs with a chewy roll, little glass dishes of mustard and fresh horseradish, and perhaps a beer or two, they never tasted better than in Vorarlberg. For me, Austria's Rhine valley wouldn't be the same without these hot and juicy, slightly smoky and sweet snacks, just spicy enough to suit my taste.

Although this western region encompasses only a small and remote area of Austria, the country's national cookery has long played a significant role in that of a larger sphere. For the fame and heritage of the great and extensive cuisine developed and spread by the Austrian-Hungarian Empire extended to many European countries.

A love of good living is important to all Austrians who well understand the appreciation of classical music, fine wines, and gastronomic delights. They cook as they sing, with happiness, enthusiasm, and imagination. Each dish reflects a sparkling and artistic touch. A highlight of any visit to this friendly, picturesque country in the heart of Europe is the marvelous food that can be enjoyed in charming cafés, coffeehouses, informal restaurants, and pastry shops featuring traditional specialties.

Over the centuries, the Austrian cuisine has been greatly influenced by its neighboring countries, particularly in Central Europe, the Balkans, and, to a lesser degree, the Mediterranean and Western Europe. The German lands contributed smoked pork, sausages, and sauerkraut, and beer as a drink. From Bohemia and Moravia, ducks and geese, all kinds of dumplings and yeast pastries found their way onto the menus. The Hungarians contributed a fondness for paprika and goulashes. Italians introduced pasta, veal recipes, and some sweet and fruit preparations. From the Balkans came valuable spices, rice dishes, coffee, and paper-thin pastry for the spectacular strudels. To Poland we trace a fondness for sour cream, pickled foods, caraway as a spice, and poppy seed pastries. Switzerland was responsible for the generous use of milk, butter, and cheeses in many dishes.

The Austrians drew on the culinary traditions and foods of others but also added their own imaginative touches. The unique quality of Austrian cooking lies in the blending of all these elements, in the harmonization of ingredients, preparations, and traditions from many lands, unifying them into one cuisine. Within a very small area there is a pleasing variety of cooking and dining traditions. To eat well and often is an everyday joy, for the people truly adore eating and dining. They prepare for it, think about it, and discuss it. Exceptional experiences at the table are a way of life.

Austrian gastronomy reached its pinnacle in the kitchens of Vienna, long an important crossroads of Central Europe and the cultural center and capital of the great Austro-Hungarian Empire that existed 600 years. The culinary extravagance and luxury of meals served in the handsome palaces of the beautiful and lively city became legendary.

Today, as in yesteryear, it is delightful to dine anywhere in Austria, but especially in Vienna. Particularly inviting are the colorful and friendly restaurants starring local specialties, such as rich soups, fish from the lakes and rivers, veal, pork, and game dishes, boiled beef, goulashes, chicken preparations, noodles and dumplings, and the lavish desserts. Great stars in the gastronomy are cakes as well as sweet dumplings, pancakes, cookies, and pastries of all descriptions. It is always difficult to choose among the inviting and astounding variety of toothsome wonders.

The Viennese love their ubiquitous coffeehouses where one can sit and read or relax with a cup or two of delectable coffee, which is served in appealing variety. Also enjoyable are the little suburban taverns or houses called *hueriger*, where the atmosphere is festive and friendly, and the purpose of gathering together is to sample the new local wines (*huerigen weine*) with convivial companions.

Quite naturally many of Vienna's notable specialties and drinks are enjoyed throughout Austria. Some people believe that Austrian cooking means Viennese cooking. Yet, surprisingly, for such a small country, there are quite distinct regional differences in the cooking, not so much in the restaurants but certainly in the homes.

During my sojourns in Austria I have learned that in order to partake of the diversity of the local gastronomy it is best to plan one's eating and dining schedule. This is a particularly good idea for the rich repertoire of sweets. Sample a strudel, torte, or yeast cake with coffee in mid-morning and afternoon, and savor light puddings and enticing egg creations as desserts after the hearty meals.

Austrian cooks, of course, are world-renowned for their rich and rare pastries, which generally require a diverse selection of ingredients, as well as time and dexterity. Lesser known are light and elegant desserts based primarily on eggs, milk, butter, sugar, and flour, which are comparatively simple to make.

On dessert menus there are generally one or more dishes called *schmarrn*, which are delectable light mixtures. The word means "a mere nothing or trifle," and the desserts are based essentially on breads, rolls, semolina, or flour. They are sometimes called a pudding, a pancake, or an omelet. Another creative sweet dessert, which the Austrians call *mehlspeise* (literally "flour dish"), is a matter-of-fact name for an enticing variety of cakes.

While high-quality beer, including Fohrenburg from Bludenz in Vorarlberg, is Austria's national drink, the country also produces a good variety of red, white, and rosé wines. Fun places to enjoy them are the outdoor wine gardens with shade trees, long wooden tables and benches, or inside wood-paneled *stubens* (pubs) with similar large tables and bench-style seating. Here one dines on an array of hot and cold foods ranging from fried chicken, sausages, fruit fritters, salads, breads, various pickles and condiments, accompanied by the singing of nostalgic songs and the melodies of strolling musicians.

Austrians also are fond of a dry apple cider called *most,* and spirits such as *schnapps,* made with a variety of fruit flavors that are known as *obstler.*

Today the love of good eating and drinking continues in Austria as it has for centuries, reflecting the esteem for the art of cooking and the pleasure of dining in good company. This selection of recipes gives you the opportunity to experience a sampling of the Austrian cuisine.

APPETIZERS

In Austria appetizers called *Vorspeisen,* a word meaning "before foods," can be a few selections or a copious spread. Some are simple creations like stuffed eggs, sausages, cheeses, dainty canapes, cold meats, or pickles. An array may include filled pastries, composite salads, a variety of smoked fish, pickled herring, raw or pickled vegetables, seafood creations, or fish in marinades or sauces. Here are recipes for a few selections.

PIQUANT CREAM CHEESE SPREAD

From the Hungarians, the Austrians borrowed one of their favorite appetizers commonly called *Liptauer*. The name derives from a Hungarian soft white cheese that originated in a province called *Liptauer* or *Liptoi*. The dish is served in two ways. The first is to place a large piece of white cheese in the center of a plate surrounded with tiny mounds of chopped chives, mustard, chopped onions, freshly ground pepper, chopped anchovies, and paprika. The idea of the dish is that since the cheese has little flavor, each bite, mixed with one of the seasonings, will be different. The second version is to combine the cheese with the seasonings and serve it as a spread in the form of a mound or another desirable shape. Additional seasonings that also can be used include caraway seeds, chopped gherkins, and capers. Cream or pot cheese is a good substitute for the *Liptauer*. This is one of the many versions.

2 packages (3 ounces each) cream cheese, softened
¼ cup (½ stick) unsalted butter, softened
2 tablespoons chopped drained capers
1 tablespoon chopped chives
2 tablespoons chopped white or yellow onions
2 flat anchovy fillets, minced
2 teaspoons Dijon-style mustard
2 tablespoons paprika
Freshly ground black pepper

In a large bowl cream the cheese and butter until smooth. Add capers, chives, onions, anchovies, mustard, paprika, and pepper. Mix to blend well. Shape into a mound on a serving plate. Chill, covered with plastic wrap, for 1 hour, up to 8. Serve surrounded with thin pumpernickel slices or other dark bread. 4 to 6 servings.

FELDKIRCH EGG AND TOMATO "MUSHROOMS"

In Austria mushrooms have long been symbols of good luck. Replicas of white-stemmed mushrooms with red and white speckled caps, made of wood, glass, china or earthenware, are sold as Christmas tree ornaments, home decorations, candle holders and other various items. An edible replica that appears frequently on the appetizer table is made with hard-cooked eggs and tomatoes. It may be used as a garnish or served as an appetizer.

A good place to enjoy a variety of mushrooms is Feldkirch, a historic and charming market town with a lot of old fortifications still intact. Known for its variety of interesting dining places, including a former castle, the town also has arcaded market squares where many culinary specialties, including freshly-baked breads and cakes, are sold. Visitors from far and wide gather to celebrate at the annual wine festival in July.

4 hard-cooked eggs, shelled
2 medium tomatoes, cut in half crosswise
Mayonnaise

Cut a slice from the end of a hard-cooked egg so it will stand upright. Remove the pulp, seeds, and liquid from the tomato halves. Fit each half over an egg to form a "cap." Decorate each tomato top with specks of mayonnaise. 2 servings.

HAM CORNETS

These attractive and easy-to-prepare appetizers are filled with a mixture of favorite Austrian foods.

1 package (8 ounces) cream cheese
1 cup sour cream
1 tablespoon freshly grated or prepared horseradish
¼ cup minced chives or scallions, with some green tops
⅛ teaspoon paprika
Salt, freshly ground pepper
12 4-inch squares thinly sliced boiled ham

In a medium bowl combine the cheese, sour cream, horseradish, chives or scallions, and paprika. Season with salt and pepper. Put ham slices on a flat surface and spread with the cheese mixture, dividing equally. Roll into cornets or cone shapes. Fasten with toothpicks and refrigerate until ready to serve, up to 2 days. Sprinkle the tops with paprika, if desired. 12 servings.

MUSHROOM-HERB APPETIZER

As one of Europe's most heavily wooded countries, Austria has long had a bounty of wild mushrooms such as the large strongly flavored cepes and bright yellow delicate chanterelles. They and other fresh mushrooms figure prominently in the many superb dishes, either fried, breaded, sautéed with lemon juice, cooked with cream, or in soups and sauces. Sautéed with onions in melted butter, the mushrooms are a favorite topping for veal and pork dishes.

1 pound fresh mushrooms
3 tablespoons unsalted butter
2 tablespoons fresh lemon juice
⅛ teaspoon freshly grated nutmeg
Salt, freshly ground pepper
1 cup chopped fresh herbs (basil, tarragon, chervil, dill, parsley)
Garnishes: Tomato wedges, cucumber slices, gherkins

Wash mushrooms to remove any dirt. Cut off any woody stem ends. Slice thickly from the round sides through the stems. In a medium skillet melt the butter over medium-low heat. Add mushrooms and lemon juice. Sauté for 4 minutes. Add nutmeg. Season with salt and pepper. Mix in the herbs. Serve with the garnishes. 4 servings.

SOUPS

In Austria a luncheon or dinner customarily begins with some kind of soup. It's always a fitting introduction to the three- or four-course meal. One of the great favorites is a clear broth or bouillon based on stock made from meat or fish and enhanced with garnishes. These may consist of a single large dumpling, noodles, thin pancake strips, bread cubes, julienne strips of raw or cooked vegetables, or fresh herbs. Most of these soups are named for the kind of garnish used. *Bouillon mit eie*, for example, is clear beef broth with egg. Substantial soup of great variety is a mainstay of the everyday diet in most homes. Here are recipes for a few of them.

BEEF-VEGETABLE SOUP

Of all the great Austrian soups, the star of the repertoire is beef soup, *Rindsuppe*. It serves many culinary roles. The meat and vegetables cooked in it can be taken out and served as a meal. The broth is then strained and clarified and used to enrich other dishes or is served by itself as a clear bouillon. Served as a bouillon, any of a number of characteristic garnishes such as noodles, dumplings, julienne-cut vegetables, or an Austrian specialty, deep-fried dough-peas called *backerbsen*, are usually added. The clear broth plus the added garnish acquire the name of the latter. While there are many ways to prepare the soup, each is made with the finest of ingredients. This is my recipe.

2 to 2½ pounds beef bones, cracked
3 pounds soup beef, chuck, or other beef
3 tablespoons unsalted butter or vegetable oil
3 quarts water
Salt, freshly ground pepper
1 large yellow onion, peeled and thinly sliced
2 medium leeks, white parts only, cleaned and thinly sliced
2 medium carrots, scraped and thinly sliced
1 celeriac (celery root), pared and cubed
3 small turnips, pared and cubed
2 cups cut-up cauliflower
4 sprigs parsley
2 medium bay leaves
½ teaspoon dried thyme

Scald bones and rinse in cold water. Wipe the meat dry.

In a pot melt the butter or heat oil over medium-high heat. Add beef; brown on all sides. Add bones and water. Season with salt and pepper. Slowly bring to a simmer. Skim off any scum from the top. Reduce heat to medium-low. Cook, partly covered, 1½ hours. Skim again. Add onion, leeks, carrots, celeriac, turnips, cauliflower, parsley, bay leaves, and thyme. Continue cooking until vegetables and beef are tender, about 40 minutes. Remove and discard parsley sprigs and bay leaves. Take out beef. Cut into bite-size pieces, discarding any bones and gristle. Return beef pieces to soup. 8 to 10 servings.

GULYÁS SUPPE

In Austria a favorite home and restaurant soup is the Hungarian goulash *suppe*, richly flavored with paprika. It can be and often is a meal by itself or a midmorning snack, particularly relished in cold weather. The seasoning of the Austrian soup differs from the traditional Hungarian in that it includes caraway seeds, marjoram, and lemon rind.

6 tablespoons lard, bacon drippings, or vegetable oil
4 medium yellow onions, peeled and chopped
2 to 3 garlic cloves, crushed
3 to 4 tablespoons paprika
3 pounds beef chuck or round, cut into 1-inch cubes
2 large tomatoes, peeled, seeded, and chopped
2 tablespoons caraway seeds
2 teaspoons dried marjoram
1 teaspoon minced lemon rind
2 quarts water
Salt, freshly ground pepper
4 medium potatoes, pared and cut into small cubes

In a pot heat the lard, drippings, or oil over medium-high heat. Add chopped onions and garlic; sauté until translucent, about 7 minutes. Stir in paprika. Sauté 1 minute. Add beef cubes, several at a time; brown on all sides. Add tomatoes, caraway seeds, marjoram, lemon rind, and water. Season with salt and pepper. Bring to a boil. Reduce heat to medium-low. Cook, covered, for 1 hour. Add potatoes. Continue cooking until potatoes are tender, about 25 minutes. Serve in bowls. 12 servings.

DAMULS HERBED POTATO SOUP

Damuls, a popular summer and winter sports resort known for its rich alpine flora, was settled by farmers who came there from a nearby canton in the fourteenth century. One of the local specialties is a marvelous potato soup flavored with herbs.

2 tablespoons unsalted butter
1 medium yellow onion, peeled and chopped
5 cups vegetable broth or water
3 cups diced, peeled potatoes
1 cup grated raw carrots
Salt, freshly ground pepper
2 tablespoons all-purpose flour
1 cup sour cream, at room temperature
¼ cup chopped fresh dill or parsley

In a pot melt the butter over medium-high heat. Add chopped onion. Sauté until translucent, about 5 minutes. Pour in broth or water; bring to a boil. Add potatoes. Reduce heat to medium-low. Cook, covered, until potatoes are tender, about 15 minutes. Add carrots. Season with salt and pepper. In a small dish mix some of the hot liquid with the flour. Stir into soup. Cook, stirring, until slightly thickened. Mix in sour cream and dill or parsley. Leave over low heat 5 minutes. 6 to 8 servings.

CHICKEN-VEGETABLE POT

This nourishing and flavorful soup is a family one-meal dish that is good for lunch or supper.

1 stewing chicken, about 4 pounds
Salt, freshly ground pepper
2 tablespoons unsalted butter or 1 tablespoon vegetable oil
2 large yellow onions, peeled and sliced
12 cups water
1 bouquet garni (3 sprigs parsley, 1 bay leaf, ¼ teaspoon dried thyme)
½ pound fresh mushrooms, cleaned
2 cups cut-up mixed vegetables
1 can (6 ounces) tomato paste
½ pound fine egg noodles, cooked and drained
¼ teaspoon paprika

Wash chicken; wipe dry. Sprinkle inside and out with salt and pepper. In a pot melt butter or heat the oil over medium-high heat. Add sliced onions. Sauté until translucent, about 5 minutes. Add chicken; brown on all sides, turning carefully with two large spoons, until golden. Add water and bouquet garni. Bring to a boil. Reduce heat to medium-low. Cook, covered, until chicken is tender, about 1 hour. Remove pot from the stove. Take out chicken; cool. Cut chicken meat from the bones; cut into bite-size pieces. Discard bones and skin. Strain broth. Return it and the chicken pieces to the pot. Add mushrooms, vegetables, and tomato paste. Reheat and cook slowly, covered, until vegetables are tender, about 10 minutes. Stir in noodles; add paprika. 8 to 10 servings.

ALPINE SAUERKRAUT SOUP

In Austria's alpine regions a favorite soup, made with sauerkraut and sour cream, is drunk sometimes to alleviate the aftereffects of imbibing too liberally. Thus, the very popular dish is called "hangover soup" or "tipplers' soup." It's a welcome treat on any occasion.

¼ cup bacon fat or vegetable oil
1 large yellow onion, peeled and chopped
1 tablespoon paprika
3 cups finely chopped sauerkraut, drained
½ pound smoked sausage, sliced
Salt, freshly ground pepper
6 cups water
1 tablespoon all-purpose flour
3 tablespoons chopped fresh dill
1 cup sour cream, at room temperature

In a large saucepan heat fat or oil over medium-high heat. Add chopped onion. Sauté until translucent, about 5 minutes. Stir in paprika. Add sauerkraut. Sauté, mixing with a fork, for 1 minute. Add sausage. Season with salt and pepper. Pour in water. Bring to a boil over high heat. Reduce heat to medium-low. Cook, covered, for 30 minutes. In a small dish combine flour, dill, and sour cream. Stir into hot soup. Cook slowly, stirring, until thickened and smooth, about 5 minutes. Serve at once. 6 to 8 servings.

EGGS BAKED IN SOUR CREAM

Austrians are devotees of egg dishes flavored with mushrooms, sour cream, and paprika. This one is excellent for a brunch or luncheon.

4 tablespoons unsalted butter
¼ cup minced scallions, with some green tops
½ pound fresh mushrooms, cleaned and thinly sliced
2 tablespoons fresh lemon juice
2 teaspoons paprika
2 cups sour cream, at room temperature
Salt, freshly ground pepper
6 eggs
3 tablespoons fine dry bread crumbs
3 tablespoons chopped fresh parsley

Preheat the oven to 350 degrees.

In a medium skillet melt 3 tablespoons butter over medium-low heat. Add scallions; sauté 3 minutes. Add mushrooms and lemon juice; sauté 4 minutes. Stir in paprika and sour cream. Season with salt and pepper. Remove from stove. Spoon into a shallow baking dish. Break the eggs, one at a time, into the mixture. Sprinkle tops with bread crumbs and parsley. Dot with remaining 1 tablespoon butter, cut into bits. Bake until eggs are the desired degree of doneness, about 12 minutes. Serve at once. 6 servings.

RHEINTAL SUPPER SWEET NOODLES

One of the most scenic drives in western Austria leads through the Rhine Valley region where travelers can dine on a fascinating variety of savory and sweet noodle dishes. One favorite, made with cooked egg noodles and poppy seeds, is often served as an accompaniment to cold meats or poultry for Sunday supper.

8 ounces fine egg noodles
¼ cup (½ stick) unsalted butter, cut up
8 ounces ground poppy seeds
3 tablespoons sugar
½ teaspoon grated lemon rind

In a large saucepan cook noodles according to the package instructions. Drain; turn at once into a warm bowl. Stir in butter; mix with the hot noodles until butter melts. Have ready the poppy seeds, sugar, and grated lemon. Sprinkle over noodles. Serve at once. 4 servings.

Note: Finely chopped nuts such as walnuts or hazelnuts may be substituted for the poppy seeds, if desired.

BREAD DUMPLINGS FROM LUSTENAU

Austrians are true devotees of dumplings which they make in great variety and consume daily in large quantity. *Knödel* are made with flour, potatoes, or bread, and can include such ingredients as bread cubes, fruit, or liver. They are eaten as accompaniments to meats and for dessert. This is an interesting version that I enjoyed in the Rhine town of Lustenau, noted for its beautiful fruit trees and blossoms and Embroidery Museum. One local specialty, freshly-baked cheese bread, is sold in bakeries and restaurants.

3 cups (1½-inch) stale white bread cubes
½ cup milk
3 slices bacon, finely chopped
1 small onion, minced
2 eggs, beaten
2 tablespoons chopped fresh parsley
About 1¾ cups sifted all-purpose flour
Salt

Place bread cubes in a large bowl; cover with milk. In a small skillet fry the chopped bacon over medium-high heat until crisp; drain on paper towels; set aside. Remove all except 1 tablespoon of the drippings. Add onion; sauté until translucent, about 3 minutes. Add cooked bacon, sautéed onion, eggs, and parsley to the bread cubes. Mix well. Stir in enough flour to make a stiff dough. With floured hands, shape the dough into six balls. Drop into a large kettle of boiling salted water. Boil, uncovered, until dumplings rise to the top. Cook, covered, until tender, 10 to 15 minutes. With a slotted spoon remove to a strainer; drain. Test by tearing one apart with two forks. To serve, slice dumplings and sprinkle with melted butter, if desired. 6 servings.

FRIED CHICKEN

One of Austria's most popular specialties is *backhende,* breaded fried chicken that is enjoyed in the home and restaurants. Traditional accompaniments are a wedge of lemon and green salad with sour-cream dressing.

2 frying chickens, about 2½ pounds each, cut up
Seasoned all-purpose flour
2 to 3 eggs, beaten
Fine dry bread crumbs
Lard or other fat for frying
Lemon wedges

Preheat oven to 250 degrees.

Wash chicken pieces; pat dry. Dredge lightly with seasoned flour; dip into beaten eggs; roll in bread crumbs. Shake to remove any excess crumbs. In a fryer or large skillet, heat 2 to 3 inches lard or fat over medium-high heat. Add coated chicken pieces and fry until golden on one side. Turn over and fry on other side. Reduce the heat to medium-low. Fry, uncovered, until cooked and deep golden, about 15 minutes on each side. With tongs, remove to oven to keep warm. Serve with lemon wedges. 6 to 8 servings.

CHICKEN PAPRIKA

Paprikahühn, chicken pieces with a paprika sauce, is another popular Austrian restaurant and home specialty.

2 frying chickens, about 2½ pounds each, cut up
Salt, freshly ground pepper
About ⅓ cup unsalted butter
2 medium yellow onions, peeled and chopped
1 to 2 tablespoons paprika
2 medium tomatoes, peeled and chopped (optional)
About 1 cup chicken broth
2 tablespoons all-purpose flour
2 cups sour cream, at room temperature
3 tablespoons chopped fresh parsley

Wash chicken pieces; pat dry. Season with salt and pepper. In a large skillet, melt butter over medium-high heat. Add chicken pieces, a few at a time. Sauté, turning once, until golden brown on both sides. With tongs, remove to a platter. Keep warm. Add onions to drippings and add more butter, if needed. Sauté until translucent, about 5 minutes. Stir in paprika; cook 1 minute. Add tomatoes, chicken broth, and chicken pieces. Reduce heat to medium-low. Cook, covered, until chicken is tender, about 35 minutes. With tongs remove chicken pieces; keep warm. Scrape drippings; stir in flour. Gradually add sour cream. Cook, stirring, until thickened and smooth. Spoon sauce over the chicken. Sprinkle with parsley. Serve with dumplings or noodles. 6 to 8 servings.

Wiener schnitzel.
PHOTOGRAPHED BY TRUMIER.
COURTESY OF THE AUSTRIAN NATIONAL TOURIST OFFICE.

WIENER SCHNITZEL

In Austria it is always possible to dine on a superb selection of mouth-watering specialties called *schnitzels*, little cuts of meat, generally veal. On restaurant menus there are customarily several kinds such as *natur, pariser,* and *holsteiner,* as well as the most popular of them all, the *Wiener schnitzel.* This specialty of Vienna is described simply as a fried breaded veal cutlet, but such a noble dish should not be dismissed so lightly. The making of a perfect *schnitzel* requires careful attention and expertise. The veal should be only the best. The coating of flour, egg, and bread crumbs must be artfully added, and when cooked, should be golden and not dark. It also is important that a *schnitzel* be served immediately after cooking and never reheated.

4 large veal cutlets, 1½ to 2 pounds
All-purpose flour
Salt, freshly ground pepper
2 eggs, beaten
Fine dry bread crumbs
Lard and vegetable oil for frying
4 lemon wedges

Trim each veal cutlet neatly and make slits slantwise along the edges. Beat well with a wooden mallet, being careful not to tear the flesh. Have ready three bowls filled with the following: flour seasoned with salt and pepper, the beaten eggs, and fine dry bread crumbs. Dip each cutlet first in flour and shake off any surplus. Then dip in beaten egg; and lastly in bread crumbs. Again shake off any surplus. In a large skillet heat enough lard and oil of equal proportions to be ½ inch deep over medium-high heat. When hot, add cutlets and fry, 1 or 2 at a time, until golden brown on both sides. Add more lard and oil as needed. Serve at once garnished with lemon wedges. 4 servings.

CREAMED SPINACH

This is an interesting manner of preparing a favorite Austrian vegetable, spinach.

2 packages (10 ounces each) fresh spinach, washed
    and trimmed
Salt
2 tablespoons unsalted butter
1 small yellow onion, peeled and chopped
2 tablespoons all-purpose flour
½ cup beef bouillon
1 tablespoon fresh lemon juice
2 teaspoons chopped fresh dill
Freshly ground pepper
½ cup sour cream, at room temperature

In a large saucepan cook spinach in a small amount of salted water over medium-high heat until tender. Drain and chop. Set aside.

In another saucepan melt butter over medium-high heat. Add chopped onion. Sauté until translucent, about 5 minutes. Stir in flour. Cook 1 minute. Gradually add bouillon. Cook, stirring, until thickened. Reduce heat to medium-low. Mix in chopped cooked spinach, lemon juice, and dill. Season with salt and pepper. Stir in sour cream. Heat 2 to 3 minutes. 4 to 6 servings.

BREGENZ CUCUMBER SALAD

Austria's classic salad is *gürkensalat*, cucumber salad, which is prepared in several variations. This is a basic recipe. Vinegar can be replaced with lemon juice. Omit sugar, if desired. Add garlic; garnish with paprika; or add sour cream. In Austria, this salad is served with *schnitzels* or other veal dishes as well as pork and poultry.

2 medium-size cucumbers
Salt
3 tablespoons white vinegar
3 tablespoons olive oil
1 teaspoon sugar
Freshly ground white pepper
2 tablespoons minced chives, fresh dill, or parsley

Peel cucumbers, cut off ends, score lengthwise with a fork, and, slice thinly. Put in a colander and sprinkle with salt. Allow to stand 30 minutes; drain well. Turn into a serving dish. Add vinegar, oil, and sugar. Season with salt and pepper. Refrigerate 2 hours, up to 4. Serve garnished with chives, dill, or parsley. 4 to 6 servings.

RED-WHITE COLESLAW

A colorful and tasty salad made with green and red cabbages is good served with *schnitzels* or other veal dishes.

2½ cups shredded green cabbage
1½ cups shredded red cabbage
2 tablespoons sugar
¼ cup mayonnaise
¼ cup vegetable oil
2 to 3 tablespoons cider vinegar
¾ teaspoon caraway seeds
Salt, freshly ground pepper

In a large bowl combine green and red cabbages. Stir in sugar. Refrigerate, covered with plastic wrap, 1 hour. In a small dish combine the mayonnaise, oil, vinegar, and caraway seeds. Season with salt and pepper. Add to cabbage mixture. Refrigerate, covered with plastic wrap, 2 hours, up to 6, to blend flavors. 4 to 6 servings.

HORSERADISH CREAM DRESSING

This is a superb sauce for meat, fish, or shellfish.

1 cup heavy cream
1 tablespoon fresh lemon juice
2 tablespoons wine vinegar
¼ cup grated fresh horseradish
¼ teaspoon prepared sharp mustard
Salt, freshly ground pepper

In a large bowl whip the cream until stiff. Gradually add lemon juice and vinegar. Fold in horseradish and mustard. Season with salt and pepper. Serve at once. Makes about 2¼ cups.

CAPER SAUCE

This is an appealing sauce for veal or poultry.

¼ cup (½ stick) unsalted butter
3 tablespoons all-purpose flour
1½ cups beef bouillon
⅓ cup light cream
2 tablespoons drained capers
Salt, freshly ground pepper

In a medium saucepan melt butter over medium-high heat. Stir in flour. Gradually add bouillon. Cook, stirring, until thickened and smooth. Add cream and capers. Season with salt and pepper. Cook for 1 minute. Makes about 1¾ cups.

CANARY'S MILK

This is a vanilla-flavored dessert sauce with a colorful name to serve over cakes or puddings.

1 cup light cream or milk
1 egg yolk
¼ cup sugar
½ teaspoon vanilla extract

In top of a double boiler combine the cream or milk, egg yolk, and sugar over hot simmering water. Beat mixture until thickened and foamy. Stir in vanilla. Remove from the heat. Serve hot or cold with desserts. Makes about 1½ cups.

LINZERTORTE

A handsome, lattice-top cake called Linzertorte, named after the town of Linz on the Danube River, is certain to be found in homes and cafés throughout Austria. It's a beloved specialty for afternoon tea and makes an excellent dessert.

¾ cup (1½ sticks) unsalted butter, softened
¾ cup granulated sugar
2 egg yolks
1½ cups finely ground hazelnuts or almonds
2 teaspoons grated lemon rind
1½ cups all-purpose flour
½ teaspoon ground cinnamon
⅛ teaspoon ground cloves
1 cup raspberry or strawberry preserves
Confectioners' sugar (optional)

In a large bowl cream the butter and granulated sugar, beating until light and fluffy. Add egg yolks; mix to blend well. Stir in nuts and lemon rind. Into a medium bowl sift the flour, cinnamon, and cloves. Stir a little at a time into the creamed mixture. Mix well. Refrigerate, covered, for 1 hour. Preheat oven to 375 degrees. Spoon ¾ of the mixture into a 9-inch round cake pan with a removable bottom, spreading evenly. Spoon preserves over the top. Roll out the remaining ¼ of the dough and cut into 8 strips, each about ⅓ inch wide and of varying lengths. Arrange over preserves to make a lattice. Bake until crust is golden and tender, about 50 minutes. Cool on a wire rack. Remove from the pan. Dust top with confectioners' sugar, if desired. To serve, cut into wedges. 6 to 8 servings.

SALZBURGER NOCKERLN

Quaint, colorful, and friendly Salzburg, "salt castle," is noted for its Baroque beauty; annual Music Festival honoring the city's famous son, Wolfgang Amadeus Mozart; and fine dining. Salzburg's most famous creation, *Salzburger Nockerln*, is a sweet souffle made of egg whites, beaten stiff, with sugar, milk, and flour. Created over 270 years ago by a chef in the Hohensalzburg Palace, it is said that there are as many recipes for the dessert as there are people in the city.

Major variations in the preparation concern the number of eggs (from 3 to 10), the type of flavoring and the method of cooking—on top of the stove, baked, or a combination of both. The latter, I believe, is preferable.

1 tablespoon unsalted butter, softened
½ cup milk
1 to 2 tablespoons granulated sugar
½ teaspoon vanilla
4 large eggs, separated
3 tablespoons confectioners' sugar, plus additional for dusting
1 teaspoon all-purpose flour

Preheat oven to 375 degrees.

Butter a square or oval 8-or 9-inch baking dish. Add milk, granulated sugar, and vanilla. Put in oven for 5 minutes.

Meanwhile, beat egg whites in a large bowl until soft peaks form. Add confectioners' sugar, 1 spoonful at a time, beating after each addition, until mixture is thick and glossy. In a small dish combine the egg yolks and flour. Add to egg white–sugar mixture. Remove heated milk mixture from the oven. With a spatula, drop in three large mounds of egg mixture, making them wide and high. Return to heated oven for 8 to 10 minutes, or until outside is golden and puffed and inside is soft and creamy. Dust with confectioners' sugar. Serve at once. 6 servings.

EMPEROR'S PANCAKE

A favorite Austrian dessert called *kaiserschmarrn,* often translated as the kaiser's or emperor's "nothing" or "nonsense," was created for Franz Joseph I who had a delicate stomach. Trapped by a snowstorm during a hunting trip and short of supplies, a cook was able to appease the emperor's hunger with the light creation made with a few simple ingredients. Ever since, this has been a favorite Austrian specialty that is made in several variations. Some recipes include rum or brandy. It is often served with a side dish of stewed plums or other fruit.

3 tablespoons raisins
¼ cup light rum
4 large eggs, separated
2 tablespoons granulated sugar
1 cup all-purpose flour
⅛ teaspoon salt
2 cups milk
3 to 4 tablespoons unsalted butter
Confectioners' sugar

In a small dish soak raisins in rum. In a large bowl beat egg yolks and granulated sugar until light and creamy. Sift in flour and salt, adding alternately with milk. Mix until smooth. Add raisins and rum. In a large bowl beat egg whites until stiff enough to form soft peaks. Fold into the batter to combine well but do not over-fold.

In an 8-inch heavy skillet or omelet pan heat 1 tablespoon butter over medium heat. Pour in half the batter and cook 4 to 5 minutes, until golden and puffed. Turn out onto a warm plate. Rebutter pan. Return pancake to pan to cook uncooked side until golden and done. With two forks cut into shreds and remove to a warm pan. Heat more butter and cook remaining batter the same way. Remove also to a warm plate. Serve at once sprinkled with confectioners' sugar and a side dish of stewed plums or other fruit, if desired. 4 servings.

AUSTRIAN WINES

By tradition Austria is a wine-drinking country and once vineyards covered a great many acres. Now viticulture is confined to four main wine districts in the eastern side. These include Burgenland, along the border with Hungary; Styria in the southeast; Lower Austria; and around Vienna.

Almost all of the Austrian wines are white, refreshing, fairly dry, fruity, and low in alcohol with a good bouquet. Many of them carry names from the variety of grapes, as Riesling, Gewürztraminer, Sylvaner, Müller-Thurgau, plus such local favorites as Veltliner and Rotgipfler.

Most visitors to Austria are likely to enjoy the young, fresh white wines at typical drinking places called *Heurigen* that, from spring to early fall, consist of a garden setting with long wooden tables and benches. At other times they are in a string of wood-paneled rooms called *Stuben*. Besides carafes of wine, the *Heurigen* offer buffets with hot and cold foods such as fried chicken, sausages, cheeses, breads, and condiments. Another aspect of the Austrian wine experience is the *Keller* that in essence is a rustic tavern blended with the ambiance of a wine cellar.

Bottled Austrian wines such as Gruner Veltliner, Rhine Riesling, and Pinot blanc are available in dining places and liquor stores. Most are white but a few are red.

GERMANY

Wines, Wursts, and *Gemütlichkeit*

Traditional German table.

When I lived in Frankfurt, Germany, one of my favorite trips was to follow the Rhine River's northward flow, winding from Switzerland to the Netherlands, through marvelous German regions on both sides of the legendary waterway. Our family could enjoy historic sights, take in folk festivals, and dine on traditional fare. "Father Rhine," as Germans affectionately call the river, has a glorious past and is still loved by romantics, painters, poets, and musicians as well as travelers and gourmets. The German Rhine trips are memorable highlights of my European journeys.

To follow the great and historic river we begin at the Upper Rhine that flows from Lake Constance, or the Bodensee in German, along the Baden and Black Forest regions on the east. Then paralleling the river on the west, past rolling vineyards and pictorial wine towns, is the country's largest wine-producing area called the Palatinate (*Rheinpfalz*), once known as the "Wine Cellar of the Holy Roman Empire." Here is Germany's famed *Weinstrasse* (Wine Road), a delightful drive. Farther along, the Rheinhessen area is bounded on the east and north by the Rhine, and on the west by the Valley of the Nahe. This is before reaching a small belt of land along the north bank of the Rhine, the Rheingau, known for its hospitality and vineyards. Historians say it was Charlemagne who first recognized the viticulture potentials of the area. Called a gift of nature, it was once the world's foremost white wine region. Now only a short distance from the Frankfurt airport, it is convenient for travelers who enjoy its scenic and wine attractions.

Then we continue along the fabled Middle Rhine, the most spectacular and romantic reach of the river. In the 90-mile stretch between Mainz and Koblenz, the Rhine has cut a deep and winding gorge between the steep slopes. Here are legends of historical and mythical figures, some forty castles, ancient cities, the legend-haunted rock called Loreley or Lorelie, and even a Mouse Tower, Der Mauseturm, that stands on an island and once served as a signal for ships passing through the difficult waterway. The Lower Rhine goes past quaint villages and the cosmopolitan cities of Bonn and Cologne.

By the mid-1800s the Rhine regions of Germany had become a travel experience, a place to visit or to make the object of a special trip. The introduction of steamship service on the river about this time helped boost the Rhine's popularity. While a taste for the picturesque enhanced its appeal, so did the publication of travel books. It was Karl Baedeker, a young German bookseller, who, after buying a small publishing firm with assets including a Rhine guide, revised and reissued a *Handbook for the Rhine* in 1829. Later, noting the success of English guide books for Continental travel, published by John Murray, Baedeker launched his now-famous series of detailed tomes that include a dark red cover, maps, and a system of rating attractions with stars. An English translation of the Rhine book appeared in 1861. With the growing popularity of European travel in the United States and success of the Baedeker and Murray books, *The Tourist in Europe* was published in New York in 1838. But it was the publication of Mark Twain's *A Tramp Abroad* in 1880 that really spread the word about the Rhine's glories to potential American travelers.

As one writer extolled, the Rhine "offered all the requirements of picturesque beauty, with a touch of Gothic throne in, as travelers floated slowly along the sinuous course of the river past countless ancient castles and ruins perched on wooded hills overlooking the water."

Contemporary travelers aboard sleek ships, cruising up and down the waterway, may find it difficult to realize that the thriving lands on either side of the river once were occupied by the ancient Celts who formed farming settlements. Yet, the early tribes of this area were nomadic warriors and hunters who were dubbed Germans by the ancient Romans. The first full account of the manners and customs of these people was in the book, *Germania*, written in the first century A.D. by the Roman historian Cornelius Tacitus who remarked that they subsisted primarily on simple fare with an emphasis on "fruits, nuts and sour milk."

Except for a comparatively small southern area of rolling hills, what is known as the Rhineland lies within a northern "civilized landscape" where the Romans planted the first grape cuttings and people were inspired to vitalize agriculture and domesticate animals. The cookery reflects this important heritage, the closeness to the great river, and, because of its central location, the culinary traditions of surrounding countries. Although the early German diet was limited in range, it was adequate, relying on good, nutritious foods and basic agriculture. The cooks had an intuitive way of dealing with what they had and made creative dishes with their bounty. Thus the substantial soups and stews had particular character and inventiveness. Even the roast haunches and lesser cuts of game and meat were imbued with distinction and appeal.

Essentially, the Germans were hearty eaters who established a propensity for meats, which are all-important to the diet. They were particularly fond of the wild boar, the ancestor of the pig, which has remained the supreme favorite over the years. The repertoire of German *schwein*, or pork creations, has long been one of the most imaginative and extensive in the world. Cooks created a seemingly endless number of substantial and inviting dishes to make use of every part of the pig.

It was probably from the Romans that the Germans learned the technique of making sausages—and certainly these savory foods became very important to the cuisine. Perhaps the Germans can be credited with originating as many as 300 kinds of sausage. The extraordinary variety displayed in butcher shops and grocery stores attests to the ingenuity of many persons who have combined minced or ground meats with spices, and sometimes other foods, to fashion this traditional fare.

Since ancient times the Germans also have been fond of their great abundance of game readily available in the deep forests. For centuries inventive cooks have practiced the techniques of transforming game into unusual and delectable gastronomic creations that are served in the homes and restaurants. Also important for the everyday diet was the abundant supply of fish from the Rhine and its tributaries. The fine species, particularly salmon, trout, and carp from the inland lakes, rivers, and streams are still inviting fare.

Other important basic foods are grains. The Germans have long relied on barley and rye to make gruels, porridges, and breads. Rye became the great favorite for making a wide variety of dark whole grain breads, which over the centuries have been standard in the family diet. Wheat, grown in later years, was used for making lighter white breads, dumplings, noodles, and pancakes, all food beloved by Germans. They also are fond of dried lentils, beans, and both yellow and green peas, which are used extensively in the rib-sticking nourishing thick soups and stews.

A New World gastronomic gift, the potato or *kartoffel*, a name taken from the Latin for "little truffle," became the king of the German vegetables and one of the country's most important food products. The potato was not accepted as fit for human consumption until the late 1700s, and then only under pressure or as an act of desperation during severe food shortages. Fortunately, the South American import thrived in the northern soil, and the Germans became so fond of the potato that their cooks devised an incredible assortment of nourishing potato dishes—salads, pancakes, dumplings, and soups, among many others.

An outstanding early characteristic of German cookery was an extraordinary predilection for fresh and dried fruits in a wide range of dishes. Such favorites as apples, cherries, pears, and plums are still used imaginatively in great quantity for cold soups, meat and vegetable creations, salads, and baked goods. Although very important as a sweetener, the fruits also are used as accompaniments for meats, poultry, and game, as well as toppings for such popular dishes as dumplings and pancakes.

Perhaps this German reliance on fruit came about because their supply of vegetables was extremely limited to a few kinds, such as the root varieties, turnips, beets, carrots, and particularly cabbage. No cooks have devised as many ways for preparing and serving fermented cabbage, or sauerkraut, an acquisition from the Slavs. In fact, the eating of this flavorful food is almost a way of life. It seems as if sauerkraut, in some variation, flavored with caraway seeds, juniper berries, fruits, wine, or beer, appears on just about every German plate.

Since medieval times German cookery was enhanced with foods from the Near and Far East. Capers and mustard became characteristic flavorings for sauces and fish, and such spices as anise, cardamom, and ginger were freely used in a wide number of baked goods. Although the oldest and most famous repertoire of cakes and cookies were flavored with honey, the *Konditoreien* (pastry shops) have long featured a wealth of mouth-watering goodies made of spices, fruits, and nuts. Coffee became the national beverage and the pleasure of enjoying coffee and sweets is an established way of life.

The Germans love to eat at home with family and friends, but they also are devoted to the pursuit of dining out in their numerous public eating houses. For snacks, there are indoor and outdoor cafés, as well as vendors plying the streets. Even at the markets or in the stores it is always possible to find some aromatic hot sausages or sandwiches, and an assortment of cold foods, including smoked fish. Also, at any time during the day or evening it is customary to pause at a *Keller* for a beer or two, or a *Weinstube* to sample the incomparable wines. Restaurant menus are lengthy with nourishing soups, cabbage and root vegetable dishes, richly sauced meats, and game of great variety.

It was an eighteenth-century Frenchman who praised Germany's inns for their hospitality and good food. In 1796 the unknown author of "Letters on the Germans by a Traveling Frenchman," assured his countrymen that Germany not only had numerous cheerful inns, but "their owners shirk no effort to serve their guests with zest and style." Many of these historic inns still exist. In nearly every town or city, and in most of the villages, one finds at least one old tavern, inn, or hotel with a long culinary pedigree, a history full of delightful anecdotes, furnishings, and utensils that have withstood the passage of time, and a menu featuring delectable local specialties. As a guide book to Germany's Historic Inns advises, "Good eating is an adventure, and Germany is a perfect place for even the most discriminating gourmet to explore."

The art of good cooking, meant to give pleasure, and a love of good living persists today in Germany. So does the spirit of warmth and fellowship, *Gemütlichkeit*. Fortunately, much of the cuisine remains true to the traditional eating customs established long ago, as exemplified by this selection of recipes.

VORSPEISEN

For their parties, both intimate and large, the Germans prepare attractive displays of *Vorspeisen*, "before foods" or appetizers. Generally some of the foods will be purchased in their delicatessens or stores. Others are prepared at home. Among the purchased fare may be smoked fish (herring or eel), other herring dishes such as roll mops, a variety of sausages and cheeses, thin slices of cold meats, types of pâté, pickles, and pickled vegetables. With these may also be served hot or cold salads of seafood, chicken, or meat; stuffed tomatoes; mushrooms; filled puff pastries; handsome stuffed eggs; and elaborately garnished canapes.

For a small selection of appetizers an attractive platter can be made with the following:

1. Roll ham slices around canned white asparagus. Garnish the top of each roll with one stalk of asparagus and a strip of pimiento.
2. Fill small tomatoes with ham, cheese, or liver pâté, and dot the caps with bits of mayonnaise. Replace caps over the fillings.
3. Arrange thin slices of salami, cold meats, and cheese, overlapping each other, and garnish with pickles.
4. Cut any kind of smoked or canned fish into bite-size pieces and garnish with chopped dill and lemon wedges.

Serve with the platter two or more kinds of white and dark bread, pats of butter, and mustard.

SPEYER MUSHROOMS ON TOAST

Speyer, located on the western bank of the Rhine in the Palatinate region, was one of the great cities of the Holy Roman Empire, probably founded in Celtic times. Here the major attractions include the majestic eleventh-century Kaiserdom, one of the Europe's finest Romanesque cathedrals with six imposing towers, and the Palatinate Historical Museum that includes an exceptional Wine Museum with pruning hooks, strainers, glass bottles and wooden casks, and other exhibits.

Mushrooms are favorite German fare, served in a number of inviting dishes for *Vorspeisen*. This variation of *champignon-schnitte,* a slice of bread topped with richly sauced mushrooms, is a good appetizer or first course.

In Speyer the Wirtschaft zum Alten Engel, a historic cellar tavern in the heart of the city, is a good place to enjoy regional dishes including those made with mushrooms.

1 pound fresh mushrooms
½ cup (1 stick) unsalted butter
Juice of 1 large lemon
¼ cup all-purpose flour
1½ cups rich brown gravy
½ cup dry white wine
⅛ teaspoon freshly grated nutmeg
Salt, freshly ground pepper
8 toasted firm white bread slices, crusts removed
Chopped fresh parsley

Wash mushrooms to clean them. Cut off any tough stem ends. Cut crosswise into thin slices.

In a large skillet heat butter and lemon juice over medium-high heat. Add sliced mushrooms. Sauté 2 minutes. Stir in flour and ¾ cup gravy. Cook, stirring, 1 minute. Add remaining ¾ cup gravy, white wine, and nutmeg. Season with salt and pepper. Cook, stirring, 1 or 2 minutes, until the mixture is thickened.

Cut toast into triangles and arrange on a serving dish. Spoon the hot mushroom mixture over them. Sprinkle with parsley. Serve at once. 4 to 6 servings.

ROLL MOPS

This is one of the most popular German appetizers that is commonly sold in stores but can be prepared at home.

12 salt herrings
Dijon-style mustard
2 tablespoons capers
2 large yellow onions, peeled and thinly sliced
3 large dill pickles, cut into 12 pieces
1½ cups cider vinegar
1 cup water
2 teaspoons sugar
6 peppercorns
6 juniper berries
2 small bay leaves

In a large bowl soak herring in cold water to cover for 24 hours, changing the water 3 or 4 times. Drain. Remove any bones from the herring; wash and wipe dry. Lay a fillet, skin side down, on a flat surface. Spread with mustard. At one end, place ½ teaspoon capers, some onion slices, and 1 piece of pickle; roll up. Secure with toothpicks.

Repeat for each fillet. Place in layers in a large, nonmetallic bowl or dish.

In a large saucepan combine the vinegar, water, sugar, peppercorns, juniper berries, and bay leaves over medium-high heat. Bring to a boil. Reduce heat to medium-low. Cook, uncovered, 5 minutes. Remove from heat; cool. Pour over the herring. Add any remaining onion rings. Refrigerate, covered with plastic wrap, 4 to 6 days. Drain. Serve on individual plates, if desired. 6 servings, offering 2 to each person.

KOBLENZ ASPARAGUS SOUP

Located at a geographic nexus known as the "the corner of Germany," Koblenz is the cultural and business center of the middle Rhine region. Because of its strategic position, the meeting point of three rivers, the Rhine, Moselle, and Lahn, it was from earliest times of great military importance. In 9 B.C. a Roman castle was built, around which developed the flourishing Roman town, Confluentes. Today's city, located on the Rhine's west bank, has a great many points of interest, ranging from the oldest restaurant, Deutscher Kaiser in the Old Town, to the Weindorf, a wine "village" with music and cafés, and the Rheinanlagen, a six-mile promenade along the river.

In Germany this soup is traditionally made with the highly prized white asparagus called *spargel.* The Germans began growing the vegetable in the 1700s and it has been a national culinary treasure ever since. There are many great dishes, including soups, made with the delectable stalks. Green asparagus, however, can be a good substitute.

1 pound fresh white or green asparagus
2 teaspoons sugar
Salt
1 cup light cream
2 tablespoons unsalted butter, softened
2 tablespoons all-purpose flour
2 egg yolks, lightly beaten
⅛ teaspoon freshly grated nutmeg
Freshly ground pepper
3 tablespoons chopped fresh parsley

If white asparagus is used, it must be peeled from just below the tip to the base. For green asparagus, trim off the scales and any tough stalk ends. Wash well and cut into 1-inch pieces, reserving the tips.

In a large saucepan bring 5 cups water to a boil over medium-high heat. Add asparagus pieces and sugar. Season lightly with salt.

Reduce heat to medium-low. Cook, covered, until asparagus is tender, about 12 minutes. In a food processor, process the cooked asparagus and liquid. Turn into a large saucepan. Over medium-high heat, heat slowly. Add cream. In a small bowl combine softened butter and flour until smooth. Form into small balls. Drop into the hot soup. Cook, stirring, until thickened. In a small dish mix 2 or 3 tablespoons of the hot soup with the egg yolks; return to hot soup. Meanwhile, cook asparagus tips separately in salted boiling water to cover until just tender. Add with nutmeg and pepper to hot soup. Season with salt. Leave on stove only a few minutes, stirring. Serve garnished with parsley. 8 servings.

BEER SOUP

Soups made with light or dark beer have long been popular in Germany, where they are prepared in several variations. They may be clear or creamy, hot or cold, and can be flavored with eggs, cream, lemon juice, sugar, sour cream, or spices. Some of the soups include slices or cubes of pumpernickel or rye bread. While beer soups are not to everyone's taste, there are many people who do like them. This is one good version.

    2 cans (12 ounces each) beer
    1 tablespoon fresh lemon juice
    2 teaspoons sugar
    1 small stick cinnamon
    1 or 2 whole cloves
    1 or 2 teaspoons cornstarch

In a large saucepan combine the beer, lemon juice, sugar, cinnamon, and cloves over medium-high heat. Bring to a boil. In a small dish moisten cornstarch with a little cold water. Stir into the hot soup. Reduce heat to medium-low. Cook, stirring, 3 or 4 minutes. Remove from the stove. Remove and discard cinnamon stick and cloves. Serve hot. 4 servings.

FARMERS' BREAKFAST

In Germany breakfast, *frühstuck*, is a hearty meal that is often followed by a second one in midmorning. This favorite potato-egg dish is called farmers' breakfast, *Bauernfrühstuck*. Serve for a weekend brunch or lunch.

6 slices thin bacon, cut in small pieces
1 medium yellow onion, peeled, and chopped
3 medium potatoes, cooked, peeled, and cubed
Salt, freshly ground pepper
2 tablespoons chopped fresh parsley
6 eggs, beaten

In a large skillet fry the bacon until crisp over medium-high heat. Remove from pan; drain on paper towels. Pour off all except 3 tablespoons of the bacon fat. Add chopped onion; sauté until translucent, about 5 minutes. Stir in potato cubes. Cook until golden. Season with salt and pepper.

Meanwhile, in a medium bowl combine the cooked bacon, parsley, and eggs. Season with salt and pepper. Mix well. Pour over the potato-onion mixture. Reduce heat to medium-low. Cook until eggs are set. While cooking, slip a knife around the edges to let the wet egg mixture run under. When cooked, remove from the stove. To serve, cut into wedges. 4 servings.

BAD DÜRKHEIM
LENTIL-SAUSAGE EINTOPF

The thriving wine town of Bad Dürkheim on the *Weinstrasse* is known for its curative waters and vineyards. It also boasts the world's largest sausage festival, as well as Germany's greatest wine festival, in September or October when thousands of celebrants revel with music and food, especially sausages, and wine flows freely. A great and unique place to dine is the Dürkheimer *Fass*, a wine-tasting house and restaurant inside a giant wine barrel, or *fass*. Advertised as the "World's Only Restaurant in a Cask," it offers hearty regional fare. Not far from Bad Dürkheim is a historic tavern called the Weinstube Zum Käseboro (Cheese Bureau) where one dines on superb fish and game specialties.

Very characteristic and basic to the German family meal is a hearty and nourishing *eintopf*, a one-pot dish that can be a thick soup or stew. *Eintopf* creations are enjoyed amid the convivial *gemütlichkeit* atmosphere of an inn, tavern, or restaurant. This one is made with two very popular German foods: lentils and sausages.

6 slices thin bacon, diced
2 large yellow onions, peeled and sliced
2 medium leeks, white parts only, cleaned and sliced
2 large carrots, scraped and diced
1 cup diced ham
2 cups (1 pound) dried lentils, washed and drained
5 cups water
1 medium celery stalk, with leaves, diced
½ teaspoon dried thyme
Salt, freshly ground pepper
1 can (l pound) tomatoes, undrained
4 cups tomato juice
10 frankfurters, thickly sliced
2 cups broken pasta (spaghetti, macaroni, or noodles),
    cooked and drained
3 tablespoons cider vinegar
⅓ cup chopped fresh parsley

In a pot fry the bacon until soft over medium-high heat. Add onions, leeks, carrots, and ham. Sauté 5 minutes. Add lentils, water, celery, and thyme. Season with salt and pepper. Bring to a boil. Reduce heat to medium-low. Cook, covered, until most of the liquid has been absorbed and lentils are soft, about 30 minutes. Add tomatoes, tomato juice, frankfurter slices, and pasta. Cook another 10 minutes. Stir in vinegar. Remove from the stove. Serve sprinkled with parsley. 8 to 10 servings.

SAUERBRATEN

Sauerbraten, a marinated pot roast, is a typical Rhine dish that has a misleading name, "sour pot roast." For although the meat is marinated in a tart liquid, the resulting richly flavored dish is a pleasure to savor. In Germany there are many recipes for preparing sauerbraten, some of which differ according to their region of origin.

> 4- to-5 pound boneless beef roast (bottom round, rump, or chuck), trimmed of fat
> 1 cup dry red wine
> 1 cup red wine vinegar
> 2 cups cold water
> 1 large yellow onion, peeled and thinly sliced
> 1 medium bay leaf
> 8 peppercorns, bruised
> 4 whole cloves
> 4 parsley sprigs
> Salt
> 2 tablespoons all-purpose flour
> Freshly ground pepper
> 3 tablespoons lard or other fat
> 1 cup finely chopped onion
> 1 medium carrot, scraped and diced
> 8 gingersnaps, crumbled

Put the beef in a large kettle or bowl. In a medium saucepan combine the wine, vinegar, water, onion, bay leaf, peppercorns, cloves, and parsley. Season with salt. Bring to a boil over medium-high heat. Pour over the beef and cool. Refrigerate, covered, for 1 to 3 days, turning at least once each day. Take the meat from the marinade; pat dry. Strain the marinade and reserve. Rub the meat with flour seasoned with salt and pepper.

In a pot melt the lard or fat over medium-high heat. Add beef; brown on all sides. With 2 large spoons remove to a plate. Add chopped onion and carrot to the drippings. Sauté for 5 minutes. Add 3 cups of the reserved marinade. Bring to a boil over high heat. Return meat to the pot. Cook, covered, until the meat is tender, about 2 hours. Remove meat to a warm platter. Bring remaining liquid and drippings to a boil. Add crumbled gingersnaps. Cook until thickened, 1 or 2 minutes. Remove from the heat. To serve, slice the meat. Pour the sauce over it or serve separately. 6 to 8 servings.

BRATWURST IN BEER

The small whitish pork sausage called Bratwurst originated in Nürnberg, the principal city of Franconia. Here and in Rhine locales the crisp spicy sausages are grilled over a wood fire that permeates the meat, and served with pepper-flavored sauerkraut and freshly grated horseradish. They are also cooked in other ways, often fried and served with fried potatoes, or, as in this recipe, in beer.

12 bratwurst
1 tablespoon unsalted butter
2 medium yellow onions, peeled and chopped
1 cup beer
Salt, freshly ground pepper
1 tablespoon all-purpose flour
2 tablespoons chopped fresh parsley

Put bratwurst in a medium saucepan. Cover with boiling water. Cook over medium-high heat 3 minutes; drain.

In a large skillet melt the butter over medium-high heat. Add the bratwurst and brown on all sides. Remove to a warm place. Pour off all except 2 tablespoons of the fat. Add chopped onions. Sauté until translucent, about 5 minutes. Return sausages to the skillet. Add the beer. Season with salt and pepper. Reduce heat to medium-low. Cook, covered, for 15 minutes. Remove bratwurst to a warm platter. In a small dish mix the flour with a little water. Stir into the hot liquid in the skillet. Cook, stirring, until it forms a thick sauce. Add the parsley. Pour over the bratwurst. Serve with mashed potatoes. 4 servings.

MEATBALLS IN CAPER SAUCE

These flavorful meatballs, *Königsberger Klops*, are generally made with ground pork but may include other meat such as beef or veal. Piquant with lemon juice and capers, they originated in the Baltic seaport of Königsberg, once an important German city that is now a part of Russia. Serve for an informal winter supper or luncheon.

2 pounds ground pork or mixture of pork, veal, and beef
1½ cups soft bread crumbs
½ cup milk
2 eggs
1 medium yellow onion, peeled and chopped
3 flat anchovy fillets, drained and minced
Freshly ground pepper
4 cups beef bouillon
3 tablespoons unsalted butter
3 tablespoons all-purpose flour
Juice of 1 large lemon
3 tablespoons capers, drained
Salt

In a large bowl thoroughly combine the pork or meat mixture, bread crumbs, milk, eggs, onion, and anchovies. Season with pepper. With floured hands shape into 2-inch balls.

In a large saucepan bring bouillon to a boil over medium-high heat. Add meatballs. Cook, uncovered, until meatballs rise to the top, about 15 minutes. With a slotted spoon, remove from liquid to a pie plate; keep warm. Strain liquid and reserve.

In a large saucepan melt butter over medium-high heat. Stir in flour; blend well. Gradually add 3 cups strained liquid; cook slowly, stirring constantly, until thickened and smooth. Add lemon juice, capers, and meatballs. Season with salt and pepper, if desired. Heat 5 minutes. 6 to 8 servings.

PORK–RED CABBAGE STEW

A basic German way with cooking is to combine the flavors of sweet and sour in dishes such as this typical stew. Pork and red cabbage, a favorite vegetable, are cooked with vinegar and sweetened with sugar and currant jelly to make piquant flavors that Germans love.

3 tablespoons lard or shortening
1 large yellow onion, peeled and chopped
2 pounds lean boneless pork, cut into 1½-inch cubes
1 bay leaf
3 whole cloves
Salt, freshly ground pepper
1 medium red cabbage, cleaned and finely shredded
2 tart apples, peeled, cored, and cubed
½ cup wine vinegar
3 tablespoons sugar
3 tablespoons currant jelly

In a large saucepan heat the lard or shortening over medium-high heat. Add onion. Sauté until translucent, about 5 minutes. Add the pork and brown on all sides. Add the bay leaf and cloves. Season with salt and pepper. Add enough water to cover the ingredients. Reduce the heat to medium-low. Cook, covered, for 1 hour. Add cabbage and apples and more water, if needed. Continue to cook until the cabbage is tender, about 30 minutes. Add vinegar, sugar, and jelly during the last 10 minutes of cooking. 6 servings.

HEAVEN AND EARTH

Himmel und Erde, a simple combination of potatoes and apples, is a specialty of the Rhineland that is eaten traditionally with crisp slices of pan-fried blood sausage. It is an old farm dish that is surprisingly good.

2 pounds (6 medium) potatoes, washed and peeled
Salt
4 tart apples, cored, peeled, and quartered
1 tablespoon unsalted butter
Pinch of sugar
Freshly ground pepper
¼ pound bacon, chopped and cooked

In a medium saucepan cook the potatoes in boiling salted water over medium-high heat for 15 minutes. Drain off most of the water. Add apples; cook until tender, about 10 minutes. Drain; turn potatoes and apples into a large bowl. Mash. Add butter and sugar. Season with salt and pepper. Turn into a serving dish. Sprinkle with cooked bacon. 4 servings.

SAUERKRAUT SALAD

Sauerkraut, a part of the German way of life, is healthful, rich in vitamins and phosphorous, calcium and iron. An ancient food, sauerkraut dates back to the building of the Great Wall of China when laborers ate it to combat deficiency diseases arising from a diet consisting primarily of rice. Invading Tartars introduced sauerkraut to Eastern and Central Europe where it became a staple food, used in many dishes, including salads.

This one is one of them.

2 cups sauerkraut, chopped and drained
1 medium yellow onion, peeled and chopped
¾ cup chopped green pepper
½ cup chopped scraped carrots
⅛ teaspoon mustard seeds
⅛ teaspoon celery seeds
1 tablespoon vegetable oil
½ cup mayonnaise
1 tablespoon sugar
Freshly ground pepper

In a large bowl combine the sauerkraut, chopped onion, green pepper and carrots. Mix in the mustard and celery seeds, oil, mayonnaise, and sugar. Season with pepper. Refrigerate, covered, 1 hour, up to 6, to blend flavors. 4 to 6 servings.

PURÉED CELERY ROOT

Celery root, or celeriac, a gnarled and knobby brown root vegetable with a flavor like celery, is widely used in Germany, served as a salad, with a cream or another sauce, or this simple preparation.

8 tablespoons unsalted butter
2 celery roots, washed, peeled, and diced
1 cup beef bouillon or water
4 teaspoons sugar
Salt, freshly ground pepper

In a large saucepan melt 6 tablespoons of butter over medium-high heat. Add diced celery root. Sauté 1 minute. Add bouillon or water and sugar. Season with salt and pepper. Bring to a boil. Reduce heat to medium-low. Cook, covered, until tender, about 15 minutes. Turn into a large bowl; mash well. Add remaining 2 tablespoons butter. Season with salt and pepper. 6 to 8 servings.

MAINZ POTATO PANCAKES

Mainz, capital of the Rhineland Palatinate, is one of Germany's oldest cities, founded in 13 B.C. as a Roman camp on the left bank of the Rhine, across the point where the Main River joins the Rhine. In the course of history it was occupied and destroyed many times. Yet, today many of its splendid historical monuments, such as the Electoral Palace, Romanesque Cathedral, and Gutenberg Museum, devoted to the life of Mainz's most famous son, Johann Gutenberg, and the history of printing, have been rebuilt or restored. It is also the most-carnival conscious city in Germany, especially famous for its grandiose pre-Lent carnival and Old Town parades. Rich in folk traditions such as an annual wine festival, the city also has a number of quaint little inns, wine houses, and taverns serving traditional food.

Kartoffelpuffer, crisp pan-fried potato cakes, are internationally famous German creations made in a number of versions. They are often served with applesauce and as accompaniments to roast pork or sausages.

    4 medium (about 1¼ pounds) potatoes, washed and peeled
    1 small white or yellow onion, peeled
    1 large egg, beaten
    2 tablespoons all-purpose flour
    Salt, freshly ground pepper
    Shortening for frying

Grate potatoes and onion into a large bowl. Drain off any liquid, pressing with a spoon to release all of it. Add egg and flour. Season with salt and pepper. Mix well. In a medium skillet heat enough shortening over medium-high heat to grease the surface. Drop spoonfuls of the potato-onion mixture into the pan. Fry a few minutes to brown. With a spatula turn over and brown on other side, adding more shortening, if needed. 4 servings.

RÜDESHEIM POTATO SALAD

Rüdesheim, the best known and most popular Rhine Valley wine town, set along the river's edge, is famous for its wines, vineyards, and boisterous Drosselgasse, a narrow cobbled lane lined with cozy wine taverns and rustic restaurants. Here one can visit wine cellars and the tenth-century Bromserburg Castle that has a wine museum devoted to the region's wine history with presses, drinking vessels, and memorabilia.

Kartoffelsalat, potato salad, is a great German favorite, prepared in several variations and eaten either hot or at room temperature, not chilled. It is served as a traditional accompaniment for sausages, pork dishes, or game.

6 medium (about 2 pounds) potatoes, washed
Salt
1 large yellow onion, peeled and chopped
⅓ cup vegetable oil
2 to 3 tablespoons wine vinegar
1 teaspoon sugar
2 tablespoons chopped fresh dill
3 tablespoons chopped fresh parsley
Freshly ground pepper

In a large saucepan boil the potatoes in their jackets in a little salted boiling water over medium-high heat until tender, about 25 minutes. Drain well; peel; and, while still warm, slice or cube into a large bowl. Add the chopped onion, oil, vinegar, sugar, dill, and parsley. Season with salt and pepper. Mix well. Cool at room temperature at least 1 hour to blend flavors. 8 to 10 servings.

FRANKFURT GREEN SAUCE

Frankfurt, Germany's leading commercial and transportation center, has been a center of civilization since time immemorial. It is where the Holy Roman Emperors were crowned, the meeting place of the German Confederation, and also the birthplace of the famous German poet Goethe. Here is the Goethe House and Museum.

Grüner sosse, green sauce, is a great specialty of Frankfurt where it is served in restaurants with hard-cooked eggs, meat, or fish. It is difficult to duplicate authentically unless one has access to an herb garden, as it is made traditionally with as many as seven or eight herbs.

½ cup olive oil
3 tablespoons white wine vinegar
¼ teaspoon sugar
Salt, freshly ground pepper
1 cup mixed chopped fresh green herbs (chives, parsley,
    dill, watercress, chervil)

In a medium bowl combine the oil, vinegar, and sugar. Season with salt and pepper. Stir in the herbs. Refrigerate, covered, 1 hour, up to 6. Serve cold. Makes about 1¼ cups.

APPLE-FILLED PANCAKES

Favorite German desserts are sweetened pancakes called *Apfel-pfannkuchen* that are embellished with such fruits as apples, plums, or cherries, and often topped with whipped cream.

6 tablespoons unsalted butter
4 tart apples, peeled, cored, and thinly sliced
2 teaspoons grated lemon rind
½ to ¾ cup granulated sugar
1 teaspoon ground cinnamon
1 cup sifted all-purpose flour
¼ teaspoon salt
1 cup milk
2 eggs, beaten
Confectioners' sugar

Preheat oven to 250 degrees.

In a medium skillet melt 4 tablespoons butter over medium-low heat. Add apple slices. Cook, stirring, until apples are soft. Don't overcook. Add lemon rind, granulated sugar to taste, and cinnamon. Mix well. Leave in the skillet over very low heat.

Meanwhile, in a medium bowl combine the flour, salt, milk, and eggs. Stir with a fork or whisk until smooth. Melt the remaining 2 tablespoons butter; add to flour mixture.

In a 7- or 8-inch lightly greased skillet over medium-high heat, add 3 tablespoons of the batter. Tilt pan at once to spread the batter evenly. Cook until underside of pancake is golden. With a spatula turn over; cook on the other side. Turn out onto a plate. Keep warm in oven. Continue cooking remaining pancakes. Spread ½ of each one with a thin layer of the warm apple mixture. Fold over and sprinkle with confectioners' sugar. Serve at once. 8 servings.

FRUIT CAKE

In German *kuchen* means "cake" and one of the most typical is a simple one that is topped with slices of fresh fruit and decorated with whipped cream. It can be served as a dessert, for morning coffee, and for afternoon tea.

⅓ cup unsalted butter, softened
⅓ cup sugar
½ teaspoon vanilla
2 eggs
1 cup sifted all-purpose flour
1 teaspoon baking powder
2 tablespoons milk
2 cups fresh fruit slices (peaches, apricots, strawberries)
Whipped cream

Preheat oven to 350 degrees. Line a 9 by 1¼-inch deep round cake pan with wax paper.

In a large bowl cream the butter and sugar. Beat until light and fluffy. Add vanilla and eggs, one at a time, beating well after each addition. Sift the flour and baking powder into the creamed ingredients, adding alternately with milk. Mix to thoroughly combine the ingredients. Turn into prepared cake pan, spreading evenly. Bake in oven until tester inserted into the center comes out clean, about 35 minutes. Cool in the pan for 5 minutes. Turn out onto a wire rack; take off the paper. Cool. Arrange fruit slices, sweetened with sugar, if desired, over the cake. Serve decorated with whipped cream. To serve, cut into wedges. 6 to 8 servings.

BACHARACH WINE CREAM

Bacharach, a name deriving from the Latin for the "altar of Bacchus," the Roman god of wine, is an idyllic Rhine wine town. A captivating maze of quaint, narrow old streets, it is noted for its pictorial houses, especially the oldest and famed Weinhaus Altes Haus, Old Wine House, built in 1368. Once a leading inn of Germany it has a cozy wainscoted tavern room with oak tables, and hand-hewn chairs. The traditional drink is Bacharach Riesling.

Weincreme can be served as a cold dessert or as a warm sauce over plain cake.

2 cups dry white wine
½ cup sugar
4 eggs, beaten
1 teaspoon grated lemon rind
1 teaspoon grated orange rind
Whipped cream (optional)

In the top of a double boiler combine the wine, sugar, eggs, lemon and orange rinds over simmering water. Cook, beating with a whisk, until frothy and thickened. Pour into serving dishes. Cool. Refrigerate, covered with plastic wrap, 1 hour, up to 8 hours. Serve topped with whipped cream, if desired. 4 servings.

Traditional Bavarian costume.

GERMAN WINES

Although Germany is famous for its extensive range of beer, the Rhine River regions are renowned for their wines. Virtually all the top vineyards, those responsible for the best wines, border the great river and its tributaries. By and large, the majority of the German wines are white and the better true ones are made from the Riesling grape. There are also good wines from the Sylvaner and Traminer grapes. One of the most successful attempts to cross the Riesling with the Sylvaner resulted in the grape known as Müller-Thurgau. Its wines are pleasing and soft but they are short-lived.

German viticulture dates from the second or third century when the invading Romans settled in the Rhine valley and introduced the rudiments of planting and caring for the grapes. Thus a great variety of vines were developed. Although German wines are made in the most northerly of vine-growing regions, the valleys are suitable for the vineyards because they are sheltered by hills protecting them from winds but allowing enough sun for the necessary ripening process.

From the beginning, the attractive landscapes of the vineyards, blending with the river and forested hills, have been noted for their unique, spectacular beauty. Anyone who has driven or sailed past them, or climbed to a height overlooking the majestically flowing Rhine to view the vineyards below, has been captivated by the dramatic appeal of the wine lands.

One of the best ways to become familiar with Germany's wine locales is to drive along the Highway of Wine, *Weinstrasse*, in the Palatinate region. From Bockenheim on the borders of the Rhine-Hesse to the "German Wine Gate" in Schweigen-Rechtenbach on the Alsace frontier, this "fairway" winds along the foothills of the Haardt Mountains for almost fifty miles, bordered on either side by vineyards, sometimes up to three miles wide.

When considering a German wine, look on the label for all the pertinent data: the vintage year, wine region, town or village, perhaps the particular vineyard, and the grape variety. Those marked *Spätlese* (late harvest) are full and rich, and those labeled *Auslese* (selection) are noble wines made from extra ripe, perfect grapes, pressed separately. *Kabinett* are superior wines that are light, usually dry, and delicate.

The greatest and most famous German wines come from the Rhinegau, cradled by the southern slopes of the Taunus Hills and with the best of climatic conditions. The Rhine runs almost due west and the vineyards, rising from its right bank, enjoy a full southern exposure. Here the stylish, mature, and most noble of Riseling wines are grown. They are both fragrant and fruity, prized throughout the world.

The Rhine-Hesse region, south of the Rheingau and west of the Rhine between Bingen and Worms, is the cradle of Germany's viticulture. When Charlemagne established his imperial residence in Ingelheim, he made it a center of learning for the study and knowledge of wine cultivation. The wines of this area range from the light, pleasant table wines to the full-bodied kinds, tops among German wine exports.

Wines from the Middle Rhine, cultivated on steep terraces all along the river from the Seven Hills past the Loreley right up to the Rheingau, are hearty, palatable Rieslings with a flower-like bouquet. In the Upper Rhine Baden region there are fresh white and red wines made from a great number of different species of exquisite grapes. Some red wines come also from the Rheinpfalz, along the Ahr, and in the villages of Assmannshausen and Ingelheim but they are light, not distinguished ones.

Although most wine festivals and fairs take place in the autumn, many Rhine villages and towns celebrate throughout the year with festive gatherings. It's great fun to join in the spirit of *gemütlichkeit* wherever and whenever you can find such an event.

ALSACE

A French-German Gastronomic Crossroads

Alsatian family with apple pie.
PHOTOGRAPHED BY J.N. REICHEL.

Over the years I've returned many times to alluring Alsace, a bountiful verdant region in the northeast corner of France, bordered by the Vosges Mountains on the west and separated from Germany by the Rhine River on the east. Each visit intensifies my desire to enjoy its many faces, from quaint medieval villages and historic vineyards to views that lift the soul. Admittedly, though, it's the culinary masterpieces and distinctive wines of this intensely French province tinged with a German flavor that really captivate me. I forget haute cuisine dishes and look for great country cooking, full of flavor, inspired by diverse regional ingredients.

All one needs is a spirit of gustatory adventure to discover and partake of innovative meals featuring *charcuterie* (pork products), velvety goose liver (*foie gras*), succulent frogs' legs, freshwater catfish, wild boar, snails, pigs' feet and cheeks, and *choucroute* (sauerkraut) in every imaginable form. Miraculously, the humble foods are transformed into dishes of utmost refinement, flavorful and satisfying. Some of the best places to enjoy this regional cooking are the *winstubs*, homey cafés or wine bars.

Fortunately, Alsace is agriculturally blessed with a bounty of excellent foods. The local cookery can draw upon beautiful fruits and vegetables from luxuriant gardens and orchards, savory game from the Vosges, fresh fish from rivers and streams, and geese, ducks, and pigs from the countryside. Jams of golden-yellow plums; onions cooked to perfection in creamy tarts; delicious pâtés and *terrines*; aromatic cheeses, such as Munster; ham cooked in pastry; saddle of hare *à la crème*; spicy sausages and smoked meat; *tarte flambée*; and delicate fruit pastries are only a few well-remembered delights.

It was the French King Louis XIV who, standing on the heights of the Vosges overlooking the plain of Alsace for the first time, cried: "*Ah! Le beau jardin!*" Ever since, the province has been known as the "beautiful garden," truly an area of great beauty, also rich in food and wine. Yet, few Rhine lands have been so ravaged and devastatingly overrun as Alsace, often the scene of battles and wars between France and Germany. Originally settled by the Celts and later occupied by Germanic tribes, the area was conquered by the Roman legions of Julius Caesar in the first century B.C. Then, in spite of invasions, political and religious conflicts, the territory of *Alsatia* flourished under the Holy Roman Empire until the seventeenth century.

In 1648, the Treaty of Westphalia ceded control of the Alsace region to France and, despite interruptions, the area has maintained a strong French connection since then. Meanwhile, however, the people developed an Alsatian language from a German dialect that is still spoken. Today, Alsace remains a fascinating kaleidoscope of contrasting French and German culture, architecture, and gastronomy.

For me, it's always a pleasure to dine in Strasbourg, the cosmopolitan capital where I find sophisticated restaurants but also rustic eating places, lively and friendly with great regional dishes. Like their German neighbors across the Rhine, Alsatians are extremely fond of sausages, pork, sauerkraut, and potatoes. But there is a notable difference in their preparation. For Alsatian *choucroute*, the cabbage is cut very fine and the ingredients are flavored with white wine, apples, and juniper berries. Roast Goose is stuffed with subtly flavored sausage, and chicken dishes include Riesling and herbs. Potatoes are treated with great reverence—fashioned into fluffy pancakes, puddings, pies, and purées, as well as a dish made with coarse potato chunks cooked to a smooth mixture with white wine, garlic, and smoked bacon.

In Strasbourg's famous neighborhood called La Petite France, noted for its old timbered homes with steep roofs and carved wooden façades, narrow cobbled streets, canals with stone and wooden bridges, and lively *winstubs,* I usually dine on a wide range of authentic Alsatian fare. One of my favorites is a beloved family casserole, *Baeckaoffa* or *Backeoffe* ("baker's oven"), made with vegetables and layers of lamb, pork, and veal, marinated in white wine and spices. Here also it's great fun to visit the *charcuteries*, aromatic food stores selling large varieties of smoked meats and sausages. Alsatian butchers are renowned masters in the art of creating pork products in a land where the "noble pig" is held in high esteem. I always look for a *saucisse de Strasbourg*, made of pork and beef and resembling a frankfurter but eaten with grated fresh horseradish or sauerkraut. For desserts there are the traditional fruit-bread pud-dings, cream-stuffed pancakes, and *Kugelhopf*, a yeast-risen cake with almonds and raisins.

In Alsace a joyous excursion is a leisurely drive along the cele-brated *Route De Vin*, or Wine Route, that winds some seventy miles through a captivating landscape. Here I find the down-to-earth attractions of the region and come to grips with the importance of wine and exceptional dining.

Set back along the Vosges slopes are vineyards that produce the refreshing white wines, and nestled among them are some of the loveliest wine villages in France. With their cobbled streets, half-tim-bered houses, and storks nesting on rooftops, symbols of good luck, the picture-book towns take one back to another age. Here also names familiar on wine labels come to life: Ribeauvillé, Bergheim, Mittelwihr, and Riquewihr, among others.

Fortunately, my first Alsatian wine journey began in early October when the villages or towns are alive with chores and cele-brations evolving around the grape harvest. Like many travelers we began at Marlenheim, about fifteen miles due west of Strasbourg and next to Wangen, a typical town with winding streets and a tower-crowned city gate. From here the route winds its way south along fruitful vineyards, past wine estates, and communities built around Romanesque and Gothic churches tucked into the slopes and dramatic valleys of the Vosges, all the way to Thann.

The most famous segment of the route begins at Barr, with its Hotel de Ville, or town hall, commanding a tiny, triangular public square, and ends with the charming city of Colmar, capital of the Haut Rhin, a vineyard section between it and Selestat. It's the perfect place for sightseeing and dining. Set in a strategic position in the Rhine Valley, the city has been important both economically and mil-itarily since the days of Charlemagne. Unfortunately, it suffered con-siderable damage in World War II but many of the splendid antiquities were preserved or rebuilt.

In Colmar it doesn't take long to become captivated by the old painted and sculptured houses, shops still marked with elaborate wrought-iron signs, and wine gardens which have maintained their old-fashioned conviviality. First on every list of attractions is the world-famous Unterlinden Museum, noted for its collection of Alsatian art, sculpture, and earthenware, as well as the legendary sixteenth-century Issenheim altarpiece by the local painter, Mathias Grunewald.

For exceptional dining I favor a Colmar landmark, the renowned Maison des Têtes, "House of Heads," named for the carved heads on the façade of the lovely gabled early seventeenth-century building. Here seasonal produce and the region's bounty are impeccably served with local wines in a handsome dining room. We relished *foie gras* with truffles, *truites* (trout) *de* Vosges, succulent venison, and a heavenly fruit tart made with tiny yellow mirabelles (plums).

Not far from Colmar, but off the Wine Route, is one of Europe's gastronomic treasures, the three-star L'Auberge de l'Ill, in Illhaeusern, beautifully situated on the banks of the slow-moving Ill River. Here in an idyllic garden setting the Haeberlin brothers, Jean-Pierre and Paul, and now, his son Marc, offer a menu of innovative regional specialties that leaves every diner sublimely happy. As one farewell gesture, we toasted the courageous people of Alsace, their cooking and wines, hoping to return soon for another memorable luncheon or dinner. For Alsatians are truly devoted to their native fare, prepared with skill and devotion.

This selection of recipes is representative of Alsatian cookery, ranging from dishes created centuries ago to those enjoyed today.

ALSATIAN CHEESES

In Alsace the primary cheese is Munster (pronounced moon-STAIR or MUN-ster) that has a semisoft rich, creamy texture and strong, piquant flavor and powerful aroma.

First made in the Vosges valleys, the name derives from the village of Munster, a corruption of the word for "monastery." A good-quality cheese should have a white chalky interior and smooth, dry, russet-colored rind.

Alsatians eat the cheese in many ways, especially as an appetizer. For a Munster Plate, a large piece of the cheese is served with a large bowl of finely chopped onions, and smaller bowls of caraway, cumin, fennel, or anise seeds, that are put into or onto the cheese. Traditional accompaniments are rye bread and beer or spicy Gewürztraminer.

Another strong-flavored cheese, Gerome, named for the Lorraine village of Gerardmer, is similar to Munster but slightly larger in size. One called Le Brouere, an imitation of an ancient version of French Gruyère, has a nutty sweet flavor and bright yellow color. It is excellent for grating and goes well with fruit. Bibelkas or Bibeles, a local version of cottage cheese, is served with minced onions and garlic and chopped parsley or chives, often as an accompaniment for pancakes.

Restaurant sign in Ribeauvillé.
PHOTOGRAPHED BY MELAYE.

PÂTÉ DE FOIE GRAS

In Alsace the greatest gastronomic delicacy is *pâté de foie gras*, the succulent liver of a goose, specially fattened by forcible feeding and made into a paste or pâté. Although it is also treasured in other French areas, the renowned luxury has special significance in Alsace where the finest *foie gras* comes from geese reared to a considerable size.

According to culinary historians, the pâté was created by an eighteenth-century Norman cook, Jean Joseph Close (or Clause), who was taken by his master, the Marshal of Contades, to Alsace where he had been appointed governor. There the cook is supposed to have invented the crust-encased goose-liver pâté, perfumed with truffles. Although it was kept secret at first, the pâté gained considerable fame after Close retired in Alsace and opened a shop where it was sold and later became a world-famous export.

When buying the pâté its quality can be judged by the color and texture. It should be creamy white tinged with pink and very firm. For wines, the best to drink with the pâté are a Riesling or Traminer.

The pâté can be served in various ways as an appetizer, with bread or toast, in *terrines* or aspics, or as a garnish. An elegant salad I enjoyed in Alsace was made with paper-thin slices of the pâté placed over lettuce leaves, sprinkled with a light wine dressing, and topped with slivers of black truffles.

ONION AND BACON TART

Alsatian cooks have created a fascinating variety of delectable savory tarts that are served as appetizers, entrées or snacks. I always enjoy the traditional *zewelewai* or *tarté a l'oignon*, onion tart, made with onions and white sauce. But the beloved specialty in rustic dining places is *tarte flambée* or *flamménküche,* dubbed "Alsace's pizza," that is baked in a large oven on a long wooden spatula. Made with a rich cream sauce, onions, and bacon, the bubbly, golden tarts have a marvelous smoky taste and aroma and are best enjoyed in a rustic restaurant where they are cooked.

Here's a recipe for an onion and bacon tart that can be made easily in the home.

PASTRY FOR ONE-CRUST 9-INCH PIE
6 slices thin bacon, cut into ½-inch pieces
3 tablespoons unsalted butter
2 large yellow onions, peeled, cut in halves, sliced thinly
3 large eggs, at room temperature
½ cup heavy cream
⅛ teaspoon freshly grated nutmeg
Salt, freshly ground pepper

Preheat oven to 375 degrees.
Line a 9-inch pie plate with the pastry. Flute the edge.
In a large skillet fry the bacon over medium-high heat until crisp; drain on paper towels; set aside. Remove all drippings except 1 table-spoon from skillet. Add butter; melt. Add onion slices. Sauté until translucent, about 5 minutes. Do not brown.

Break eggs into a large bowl. Stir to blend well. Add the cream and nutmeg. Season with salt and pepper. Mix again. Add sautéed onion slices; mix well. Spoon into pastry shell, spreading evenly. Sprinkle the top with cooked bacon pieces. Bake until filling is set in the center and is golden brown in spots, about 45 minutes. Remove from oven; cool on a wire rack. Serve warm or at room temperature, cut into wedges. 6 servings.

AMMERSCHWIHR PORK *RILLETTES*

Probably each traveler has a favorite Alsatian locale and one of mine is the colorful wine town of Ammerschwihr in the Haut-Rhin. Although almost completely destroyed during World War II, it was painstakingly reconstructed to preserve its traditional ambiance. Vineyards remain its pride and joy. Here in the upstairs dining room of the hospitable gastronomic temple, Aux Armes de France, we enjoyed a marvelous repast featuring pork *rillettes* and an aromatic *choucroute garnie au faisan* (with pheasant), with, of course, Ammerschwihr wine.

Pork *rillettes*, made with shredded meat, generally pork, and packed into small pots, are a favorite Alsatian appetizer sold commercially in food shops. But they are easy to make in the home and can be kept in the refrigerator for several days to be used as desired.

2 pounds breast of pork
1 to 2 garlic cloves
½ teaspoon dried marjoram
¼ teaspoon dried thyme
⅛ teaspoon freshly grated nutmeg
Freshly ground pepper

Remove rind from the pork. Cut into pieces. In a large saucepan combine the pork pieces, garlic, marjoram, thyme, nutmeg, pepper, and ½ cup water over medium-low heat. Cook, covered, stirring now and then, until cooked, about 1½ hours. Drain and cool the meat. Remove any skin and bones. Separate meat from the fat, reserving the fat. With two forks, tear the meat into shreds and put into small earthenware or other pots. Heat the fat to melt it; pour over the meat. Chill, covered, in refrigerator, up to 8 days. Serve with crusty white bread and butter. 6 to 8 servings.

OBERNAI ONION SOUP

Obernai, a thriving Wine Route town with a colorful marketplace and sixteenth-century half-timbered and stone dwellings lining the cobbled streets, is famous as the birthplace of Alsace's patron saint, Sainte Odile. Her baptism is said to have cured her blindness.

Among all the noble dishes made with the humble and versatile onion, one of the best is a rich soup topped with toasted crusty bread and grated cheese. It's a marvelous dish any time of the day or night but is sometimes relished as a restorative in the wee hours of the morning after a night of celebrating.

3 tablespoons unsalted butter
3 tablespoons vegetable oil
1½ pounds (about 5 cups sliced) onions, peeled and thinly sliced
1 teaspoon sugar
Salt, freshly ground pepper
6 cups beef bouillon
½ cup dry white wine
6 or more slices toasted crusty white bread
About 1½ cups grated yellow cheese
3 to 4 tablespoons unsalted butter, melted

Preheat oven to 375 degrees.

In a large saucepan heat the butter and oil over medium-high heat. Add onions; sauté until translucent, about 10 minutes. Add sugar; mix well. Season with salt and pepper. Pour in bouillon; bring to a boil. Reduce heat to medium-low. Cook, covered, 20 minutes. Add wine; continue to cook 10 minutes. Ladle into earthenware or other ovenproof bowls. Top with one or more slices of toasted bread. Sprinkle generously with cheese. Sprinkle tops with melted butter. Put into oven until cheese is melted, about 20 minutes. Then put under heated broiler a few minutes, until golden and crusty on top. Serve in the same dishes. 6 servings.

SAVERNE'S VEGETABLE POTAGE

Saverne, several miles northwest of Strasbourg, and gateway to the northern Vosges, has been known since Roman times for welcoming travelers with hearty food and warm hospitality. Right in the center of town is a friendly *auberge*, or inn, on the fourth floor of the majestic red sandstone Chateau des Rohans that has a beautiful rose garden and museum devoted to local history. Saverne also has a lively weekly food market.

One of the local specialties is a thick soup-stew called *garbure* that often includes bacon, salt pork, sausages, and perhaps preserved goose, that is made in many variations. In some wine bars it's the custom for each diner, nearing the bottom of the soup bowl, to add a glass of wine to the remaining dish. This, one finds, is a good and fun addition.

2 cups (1 pound) dried navy or pea beans
2 quarts water
½ pound bacon or salt pork in one piece
4 cloves garlic, minced
4 large yellow onions, peeled and sliced
4 large carrots, scraped and sliced
4 white turnips, peeled and sliced
6 medium potatoes, peeled and sliced
1 medium head green cabbage, cored and shredded
½ teaspoon dried thyme
1 bay leaf
Salt, freshly ground pepper

In a large pot cover beans with the water. Bring to a boil; boil 2 minutes. Let stand, covered, 1 hour. Put bacon or pork in center of beans. Cook over medium-low heat, covered, for 1 hour. Add garlic, onions, carrots, turnips, potatoes, shredded cabbage, thyme, and bay leaf. Season with salt and pepper. Continue cooking until ingredients are tender, about 40 minutes. Remove bacon or pork. Cut into thin slices. Serve on the side or in bowls. Serve the soup in wide bowls over pieces of crusty white bread previously fried until golden in butter, if desired. 8 to 10 servings.

KAYSERSBERG MUSHROOM SOUP

Kaysersberg, "Caesar's Mountain," is a small historic Wine Route town built between two vine-covered slopes and crowned by the ruins of a feudal castle. It even has a stream running right down the main street and a 1514 bridge with an inscription that recommends drinking wine rather than water. Here also is the house where Dr. Albert Schweitzer was born and a museum with memorabilia retracing his remarkable life.

This cream of mushroom soup is a good first course for a company dinner.

1 pound fresh mushrooms
5 tablespoons unsalted butter
1 tablespoon fresh lemon juice
Salt, freshly ground white pepper
2 tablespoons minced shallots or scallions
3 tablespoons minced yellow onions
2 tablespoons all-purpose flour
6 cups chicken broth
1 medium bay leaf
2 parsley sprigs
¾ cup heavy cream

Wash mushrooms to remove any dirt. Pull stems from caps. Cut off any woody ends from stems; chop finely and reserve. Slice the caps. In a medium saucepan melt 2 tablespoons butter over medium-high heat. Add sliced caps and lemon juice; sauté 3 minutes. Season with salt and pepper. Remove to a plate.

In the saucepan melt remaining 3 tablespoons butter over medium-high heat. Add shallots or scallions and onions; sauté 5 minutes. Add chopped mushroom stems; sauté 2 minutes. Stir in flour. Cook, stirring constantly, for 1 to 2 minutes. Gradually add the chicken broth, stirring while adding. Add bay leaf and parsley.

Season with salt and pepper. Reduce heat to medium-low. Cook, stirring often, for 15 minutes. Strain, pressing mushrooms with a spoon to release all the juices. Return strained liquid to the saucepan. Add sautéed sliced mushrooms and drippings and cream. Leave on the stove long enough to heat through. Correct the seasoning. 4 to 6 servings.

PANADE

In Alsace a bread and broth soup is known as a *panade*. It is generally a homely dish of stock or water, or perhaps another liquid, thickened with stale slices or cubes of firm crusty white bread, to which butter, salt, pepper, and a beaten or whole egg might be added. Old recipes for a *panade*, called bread *rustique*, bread and butter soup, or *soupe rustique*, sometimes also include other ingredients such as onions, leeks, garlic, or carrots and flavorings like wine, herbs, or spices. The *panade* can be cooked on top of the stove or baked.

⅓ cup unsalted butter
2 large yellow onions, peeled and sliced
8 cups rich beef bouillon
6 thick slices stale firm white bread, torn into pieces
Salt, freshly ground pepper
⅓ cup grated yellow cheese

In a large saucepan melt butter over medium-high heat. Add onions; sauté until translucent, about 5 minutes. Add bouillon; bring to a boil. Stir in bread pieces. Season with salt and pepper. Reduce heat to medium-low. Cook, covered, 20 minutes. Stir in cheese. Cook 10 minutes longer. Serve at once. 4 to 6 servings.

QUICHE

A savory baked custard tart called a quiche and believed to have originated in Alsace's neighboring province of Lorraine, is now an internationally known dish made in many versions. Those served in Alsace include a traditional cream-and-beaten egg mixture thickly studded with bits of bacon. Some also include cheese, and perhaps a little onion. Given below is a good recipe for a typical quiche to serve for a brunch or luncheon.

The savory mixture can be cooked in a flaky crust in a metal flan ring placed on a cookie sheet, in a quiche dish, or in a regular 9- or 10-inch pie pan.

8 slices crisp fried bacon, drained and crumbled
Pastry for one-crust 9-inch pie, baked 10 minutes and cooled
4 large eggs
2 cups heavy cream
⅛ teaspoon freshly grated nutmeg
Salt, freshly ground pepper
2 tablespoons unsalted butter, cut up

Preheat oven to 375 degrees.

Sprinkle bacon bits over bottom of the pastry shell. In a large bowl beat the eggs. Add the cream and nutmeg. Season with salt and pepper. Mix well. Pour over bacon. Distribute butter over the top. Bake 45 minutes, until puffed and golden and custard is set. Cool slightly before cutting into wedges. 4 to 6 servings.

RIBEAUVILLÉ BUTTERED NOODLES

The French call the beautifully preserved, half-timbered town of Ribeauvillé, "the pearl of the vineyards." It produces some of the best wines in Alsace. Surrounded by rolling vineyards and three imposing chateaux, its ancient belfry, Renaissance fountain, and flowering, turreted houses give it a very special charm. Any time of the year, but especially in the summer and fall, its narrow main street is crowded with enthusiastic tourists who love the warm hospitality and local folklore events.

In Alsace egg-rich noodles are a typical specialty, served in soups, with a cheese or rich cream sauce, and as this favorite, *Nouilles au Beuree* or buttered noodles, sometimes studded with *foie gras*. It's a good entrée or accompaniment for game or meats.

1 package (8 ounces) wide egg noodles
5 tablespoons unsalted butter
Salt, freshly ground pepper
¼ cup grated yellow cheese (Gruyère or Swiss)

In a pot of boiling salted water cook noodles according to the package directions until just tender. Drain. In a medium saucepan heat 3 tablespoons butter over medium-high heat. Add ¾ of the cooked noodles. Season with salt and pepper. Cook, stirring with a fork, about 5 minutes. Add cheese; mix well. Remove to a serving dish; keep warm.

Meanwhile, coarsely chop the remaining cooked noodles. In a small skillet melt remaining 2 tablespoons butter over medium-high heat. Add chopped noodles. Cook, stirring, until noodles are golden brown. To serve, pour over the noodles and cheese. Toss and serve at once. 4 servings.

ST. HIPPOLYTE TROUT IN CREAM

In St. Hippolyte, another attractive Wine Route town that is north of Colmar, my favorite luncheon specialty is freshly caught trout cooked to perfection in a cream sauce. One of the area's major attractions is the fifteenth-century castle of Haut-Koenigsbourg that sits atop a high peak. Once completely demolished, it was restored early in the 1900s as a hunting lodge for Emperor Wilhelm II when the Germans controlled Alsace. Now refurbished again and open to the public, visitors may wander through its maze of dining halls and trophy rooms and enjoy the magnificent view across the Rhine River and into Germany.

4 small whole trout, cleaned
All-purpose flour seasoned with salt and pepper
½ cup (1 stick) unsalted butter
1 cup heavy cream
¾ cup chopped blanched almonds

Wash and drain the trout. Roll lightly in seasoned flour in a shallow dish. In a large heavy skillet melt ¼ cup butter over medium-high heat. Add the trout; sauté until golden-brown and flesh flakes easily with a fork, about 5 minutes on each side. Remove to a warm plate. Add cream to the drippings and let the mixture come just to a boil. Mix well. Strain the sauce through a fine sieve onto the fish.

Meanwhile, melt remaining ¼ cup butter in a small skillet over medium-high heat. Add almonds; sauté until golden, about 4 minutes. Spoon over the trout and cream sauce. 4 servings.

Alsatian family with choucroute.
PHOTOGRAPHED BY J.N. REICHEL.

CHOUCROUTE GARNIE

I first tasted an Alsatian masterpiece called *choucroute garnie*, sauerkraut garnished with a variety of smoked meats, on an autumn day in a delightful Saverne restaurant while en route to the historic city of Strasbourg. It made a memorable luncheon. Since then it has been a favorite winter party dish as it can be made beforehand and is accompanied only by boiled potatoes and mustard.

2 pounds sauerkraut
2 tablespoons bacon fat or lard
3 medium yellow onions, peeled, and chopped
2 tart medium apples, peeled, cored, and chopped
6 peppercorns
10 juniper berries or ¼ cup gin
2½ cups dry white wine
12 link sausages
6 slices cooked ham, ¼ inch thick
6 smoked pork chops or slices
6 frankfurters

In a large bowl soak the sauerkraut in cold water to cover for 15 minutes. Drain; squeeze dry between hands.

Meanwhile, in a large saucepan or pot heat the fat or lard over medium-high heat. Add onions; sauté until translucent, about 5 minutes. Add sauerkraut; toss with a fork. Cook, stirring, for 5 minutes. Add apples, peppercorns, and juniper berries or gin. Pour in white wine. Reduce heat to medium-low. Cook, covered, for 1 hour.

Meanwhile, in a medium skillet fry sausages over medium-high heat. Remove to drain on paper towels. Add with meats to sauerkraut. Continue cooking, covered, for 30 minutes longer. Discard peppercorns and juniper berries. To serve, spoon out meats onto a plate. Pile sauerkraut in center of a large warm platter. Arrange meats and sausages over the top. Serve with boiled potatoes and mustard. 6 servings.

RIQUEWIHR CHICKEN IN RIESLING

By common acclaim, the most charming and magical Wine Route town is Riquewihr, an amazing picture postcard place that, surrounded by some of the finest vineyards in France, is alive with the production and drinking of great Rieslings. A walled town of narrow cobblestone streets, where no cars are allowed, it's miraculously intact as it was in the sixteenth century. Spared devastation during the world wars, it has carefully maintained its heritage and enchanting homes. Here are little houses with sculptured beams, interior court-yards with wooden balconies, and elaborately carved doors and windows. There's a whimsical town gate called the Dolder, dating from the thirtheenth century, a town *tonnelier* (wine-cask maker), and a Tower of Thieves with ramparts and a torture chamber.

This is a local version of the French dish, *coq au vin*, chicken in wine.

6 half chicken breasts
Salt, freshly ground pepper
4 tablespoons (½ stick) unsalted butter
1 medium yellow onion, stuck with 2 cloves
1 medium bay leaf
2 cups Riesling or other dry white wine
1 tablespoon all-purpose flour
1 cup heavy cream
3 egg yolks
Pinch of grated nutmeg

Remove and discard skin from each chicken breast. Wash and wipe dry. Sprinkle with salt and pepper. In a large heavy skillet melt 3 tablespoons butter over medium-high heat. Add chicken breasts; sauté until golden brown on all sides. Add onion, bay leaf, and wine. Reduce heat to medium-low. Cook, covered, until chicken is tender, turning once or twice, about 30 minutes. Remove chicken pieces to a platter and keep warm. Strain the liquid and reserve. Reduce pan juices by cooking briskly about 5 minutes. Add remaining 1 tablespoon butter and the flour, stirring while adding. Pour in strained liquid. Add cream, egg yolks, and nutmeg. Reheat, stirring with a whisk. Pour over chicken pieces and sauce. Serve with buttered noodles. 6 servings.

FRUIT-STUFFED PORK LOIN

In Alsace the favorite meat is pork and many of the dishes made with it include dried or fresh fruits. Here's one of my favorites.

2 pork tenderloins, about 1 pound each
12 prunes, scalded and pitted
2 large tart apples, cored, peeled, and chopped
Salt, freshly ground pepper
2 tablespoons unsalted butter
About 1 cup dry white wine
2 tablespoons all-purpose flour
1 cup heavy cream

Remove any membranes from the pork and slit each tenderloin lengthwise two-thirds through to form a pocket. Fill each pocket with prunes and apples seasoned with salt and pepper. Tie with string to keep stuffing inside pockets. In a large saucepan melt the butter over medium-high heat. Add each stuffed tenderloin and brown on all sides. Add 1 cup wine.

Reduce heat to medium-low. Cook, covered, 1 hour, adding more wine, until pork is tender, about 1 hour. Remove pork to a warm platter. Cut into slices; keep warm. Skim any fat from the drippings and scrape them. Stir in flour. Cook 1 minute. Add cream and heat slowly. Serve over pork. 4 servings.

VOSGES POTATOES

This is a typical potato preparation in the towns of the Vosges Mountains.

8 medium (about 2½ pounds) potatoes, washed
Salt
3 tablespoons unsalted butter
1 medium yellow onion, peeled and chopped
3 tablespoons chopped fresh parsley
1 large egg
3 tablespoons hot vegetable oil
Freshly ground pepper

In boiling salted water in a medium saucepan cook whole, unpeeled potatoes until tender, about 25 minutes. Drain. Peel potatoes. Cut into thick slices. Set aside.

Meanwhile, in a medium saucepan melt the butter over medium-high heat. Add onion; sauté until translucent, about 5 minutes. Add potato slices and parsley. Break egg over the potatoes. Add hot oil. Season with salt and pepper. Toss gently. 4 servings.

BRAISED RED CABBAGE

Purplish-red cabbage, *chou rouge*, is a favorite Alsatian vegetable that is traditionally cooked with wine, spices, and sugar. Serve with pork or game.

1 medium head (about 2½ pounds) red cabbage
3 tablespoons unsalted butter
2 medium yellow onions, peeled and chopped
4 tart apples, quartered, cored, and chopped
3 tablespoons light brown sugar
¼ teaspoon ground allspice
¼ teaspoon grated nutmeg
Salt, freshly ground pepper
2 cups dry red wine
¼ cup red wine vinegar

Preheat oven to 350 degrees.

Cut cabbage into quarters from top to bottom. Remove any wilted outer leaves; cut out core. Wash and drain cabbage. With a sharp knife shred coarsely.

In a large ovenproof casserole melt butter over medium-low heat. Add onions; sauté until translucent, about 5 minutes. Remove casserole from the stove. Spoon onions onto a plate. In the casserole arrange layers of shredded cabbage, sautéed onions, and apples, topping each layer with a sprinkling of the sugar, allspice, and nutmeg, and season with salt and pepper. Pour in wine and vinegar. Bake, stirring once or twice, until cabbage is tender, 1 to 1¼ hours. Serve hot. 8 to 10 servings.

CREAMED KOHLRABI

Alsatians are fond of kohlrabi, or "cabbage turnip," which is prepared as a salad or creamed. It's a good accompaniment to pork dishes.

2 small kohlrabi
Salt
7 tablespoons unsalted butter
¼ cup light cream
⅛ teaspoon grated nutmeg
Freshly ground pepper
2 cups boiling water
¼ cup all-purpose flour
½ cup chopped fresh parsley

Cut off the kohlrabi leaves. In a medium saucepan cook them in salted water to cover until tender, about 15 minutes. Drain and chop the leaves. Add 3 tablespoons of butter, the cream, and nutmeg. Season with salt and pepper. Remove from the stove; keep warm.

Meanwhile, trim kohlrabi roots; peel and slice. In a medium saucepan combine the slices and boiling salted water. Cook, covered, over medium-high heat until tender, about 25 minutes. Drain, reserving the liquid. In the saucepan melt remaining 4 tablespoons butter over medium-high heat. Stir in flour; blend well. Season with salt and pepper. Add reserved vegetable liquid and cook slowly, stirring, until thick and smooth. Add the cooked kohlrabi slices and parsley. Leave on stove long enough to heat through. Serve surrounded by the cooked leaves. 4 servings.

SALADE FORESTIÈRE

Although *forestière* is a French word meaning "of or pertaining to forests," in cookery it refers to dishes that include mushrooms. Although good wild mushrooms are found in Alsatian forests, this salad is made with cultivated mushrooms. Serve as a first course or an accompaniment for poultry or beef.

2 small heads leafy lettuce, washed, dried, torn into small
    pieces, and chilled
½ pound fresh mushrooms, cleaned and sliced
½ cup extra-virgin olive oil
1 tablespoon wine vinegar
½ teaspoon dried basil
3 tablespoons chopped fresh mint or parsley
Salt, freshly ground pepper

In a salad bowl combine the lettuce and mushrooms. Add the oil; toss lightly. Add the vinegar, basil, and mint or parsley. Season with salt and pepper. Serve at once. 6 servings.

DANDELION SALAD

One of Alsace's favorite specialties is a salad made with *pissenlit*, tender young dandelion leaves, and pieces of bacon. It's often flavored with garlic. Serve as an accompaniment for meat and poultry.

1 pound small, tender dandelion leaves
4 thin slices bacon, chopped
2 tablespoons wine vinegar
2 shallots or scallions, cleaned and minced
2 garlic cloves, crushed or minced
Salt, freshly ground pepper
2 tablespoons vegetable oil

Wash dandelions; cut off roots and any damaged leaves; dry; refrigerate.

In a small skillet fry the chopped bacon until crisp; drain on paper towels. Add vinegar to bacon drippings and heat. Put dandelions, shallots or scallions, and garlic in a salad bowl. Season with salt and pepper. Add oil; toss lightly. Add heated vinegar mixture. Pour over salad ingredients; toss. Serve at once, garnished with crisp bacon. 4 servings.

PEARS IN RED WINE

Serve this typical Alsatian dessert for a company dinner.

1½ cups dry red wine
3 tablespoons sugar
1 2-inch stick cinnamon or ½ teaspoon ground cinnamon
Small piece lemon rind
6 medium firm ripe pears, peeled, cored, and halved

In a small skillet combine the wine, sugar, cinnamon, and lemon rind. Bring to a boil over medium-high heat, stirring until sugar dissolves. Add pears. Reduce heat to medium-low. Cook, covered, until pears are just tender, about 15 minutes, turning once. Remove and discard cinnamon and lemon rind. Serve pears in syrup, warm or cold. 6 servings.

APPLE BREAD PUDDING

Traditional Alsatian desserts include puddings made from stale bread and fruits, often scented with kirsch and cinnamon. This is one of them.

4 cups day-old good-quality white bread cubes
½ cup (1 stick) unsalted butter, melted
⅓ cup firmly packed light brown sugar
½ teaspoon ground cinnamon
⅛ teaspoon salt
4 cups chopped peeled tart apples
1 cup light cream or milk
2 tablespoons kirsch or apple brandy
¼ cup raisins

Preheat oven to 375 degrees.

In a large bowl combine the bread cubes, melted butter, sugar, cinnamon, and salt. In a buttered 1½-quart casserole arrange the bread mixture in alternate layers with the apples. Pour in the cream or milk and kirsch or apple brandy. Add the raisins, mixing well to distribute the fruit. Bake until apples are tender and top is golden brown, about 1 hour. Serve hot or cold with plain cream, if desired. 4 to 6 servings.

RASPBERRY PARFAIT

Alsatians enjoy a marvelous ice cream dessert called *parfait*, taken from the French word for perfect. Very often it is a type of single flavored mousse frozen in a mold. But it may also be a delicate ice served in a tall, narrow, short-stemmed glass. One of the most refreshing parfaits I ever tasted was after a superb dinner in the hotel-restaurant Aux Armes de France in Ammerschwihr. It was a simple combination of lemon sherbet covered with champagne and a little kirsch.

For an easy-to-prepare parfait, place one or more scoops of lemon or raspberry sherbet in a tall stemmed glass. Top with raspberry sauce (recipe below), a little champagne and kirsch, and whipped cream.

RASPBERRY SAUCE

2 cups fresh raspberries
2 tablespoons superfine sugar (optional)
3 tablespoons kirsch

In a food processor container combine the raspberries and sugar, if used. Blend until smooth. Strain to remove seeds. Add kirsch and mix well. Makes 2 cups.

ALSATIAN WINES

Alsace is home to the third most important wine region in France. The vineyards, which stretch along the foothills of the Vosges Mountains, from Mulhouse on the south to Strasbourg on the north, covering a strip some seventy miles long and never more than one or two miles wide, are among the most beautiful in Europe. Here the grape has been tended since the year 250. The wine district is divided into two regions, the best being that called the Haut-Rhin, between Colmar and Selestat; and the other called Bas-Rhin stretching north along the foothills and slopes between Selestat and Strasbourg.

Because it is in the north, the wine area is subject to rigorous weather conditions. Still, many geographic factors conspire to make this climate beneficial to the grape. The Vosges Mountains shelter the vineyards and at the same time, limit the rainfall. The vines, with a southern and eastern exposure, are able to get the maximum sun, while the cooler weather of this northern region allows the grapes to mature more slowly, thus developing greater fruitiness and bouquet.

Alsace is unique among French wine regions in that it labels most of its wines with the name of the grape variety used to make the wine, such as Riesling or Sylvaner, rather than with a vineyard or village. Only rarely is the name of the vineyard added as well. Some of the wines are further defined by law as *grand vin* or *grand cru*.

Alsace's wines are bottled early, usually the spring following the fall harvest. And most of them are at their best, fresh, light, and lively, green-gold, with considerable bouquet when drunk young. Some, however, also age well, retaining a degree of freshness into maturity. A wine of Alsace that is named for a grape variety must be made entirely of that grape.

Almost all the wines of Alsace are white. Among the most important are:

RIESLING: The most elegant grape of Alsace, Riesling makes a fine dry, clean, graceful wine that goes well with fish, shellfish, poultry, cold meats, and the region's sauerkraut dishes and smoked ham.

GEWÜRZTRAMINER: This is the most distinctive and individual of Alsace's wines. *Gewürz* means "spicy" in German, and this spiciness is the outstanding characteristic of Gewürztraminer. It is a delicious, fruity wine with a pungent flavor and a highly perfumed and flowery bouquet. It goes best with sausages, sauerkraut, and Munster cheese, and can be served with some desserts.

SYLVANER: This makes an agreeable, fresh, fruity, dry wine. It is best in its youth, drunk as an aperitif, and with fish.

EDELZWICKER: This name on a wine label indicates that the wine is made from a blend of different grapes such as Riesling and Sylvaner. It is a light, simple wine.

OTHER GRAPE VARIETIES: These include Pinot Blanc, Pinot Gris, and Muscat among the whites; and Pinot Noir for the red wine of Alsace. This is very light.

Festivals are an important part of life in Alsace as they are lively celebrations dedicated to all kinds of foods, from fruit to vegetables. Those honoring the grape harvests and freshly pressed wine are particularly colorful and fun. While just about every community has a wine festival, some are particularly well known. So it is best to check with the local tourist boards for advice about the locales and dates.

ALSATIAN SPIRITS

Other than wines the most celebrated drinks of Alsace are distilled spirits known as *eaux-de-vie*, waters of life, or so-called *digestifs*, which are sipped after the hearty meals. Clear, white, and potent, the fruit brandies are traditionally made entirely and only from pure, ripe fruit. Tasting one of these costly highly prized liqueurs is a great experience. For the flavor, aroma, and exquisite aftertaste of ripe fruit are delightful.

While Switzerland and the Black Forest region of Germany are also noted for their excellent *eaux-de-vie*, those of Alsace are more exotic, made from a diverse variety of fruits.

In Europe the tradition and craft of distilling dates back to the Middle Ages when monasteries produced potent fruit brandies as tonics against diseases. Thereafter distilling became widespread in Alsatian villages where farmers began making the drinks with fruits they grew or gathered, including just about anything that was available, from holly berries to forest flowers called gentiane.

The most famous of all the spirits is kirsch, a white cherry brandy of superlative flavor that is made from small, dark cherries. The next best known is *poire* Williams made from a special variety of pear. *Framboise* is a heady quintessence of raspberry that raises the process of distillation to the status of a fine art. Other notable brandies include *quetsch* (purple plum), *mirabelle* (yellow plum), and *cassis* (black currant). Although not as well known outside of Alsace, brandies are also made from apples, apricots, blackberries, and even roots and flowers.

Alsatians are also fond of a traditional drink called *marc*, a fiery clear brandy distilled from the grape pressings leftover from making wine.

An *eaux-de-vie* should be served cold in a cool balloon-shaped glass that gives the aroma a chance to develop so the drinker can better appreciate and focus on the perfume. Some people prefer a white-wine glass or small brandy snifter.

In Lapoutroie, about five miles above Kaysersberg, is the small *Musée des Eaux-de-Vie* where visitors can view exhibits of traditional distilling equipment as well as taste and buy a selection of the brandies. The drinks can also be tasted at Alsatian distilleries as well as at restaurants and wine bars.

HOLLAND

Hearty Dutch Treats

Busy Dutch café.

I first became enchanted with the beauties of the Netherlands, popularly known as Holland, during a trip with my daughter, Rae, to enjoy the annual *bloemencouso*, a flower pageant that's a marvelous rite of spring. April and early May is "Tulip Time" when the whole country seems to be filled with blazing colors. A land of impressive culture and good-natured hospitality, lovely waterways, flower-filled landscapes, and historic river towns, Holland is a proud nation with a seafaring heritage and a wealth of traditions. Outstanding among them is the cookery. Not only were we able to explore the fascinating flower culture, but also had ample time for fine dining and culinary explorations that proved to be a marvelous dividend.

Since my first visit I've returned several times to Holland, one of Europe's most extraordinary countries that has nearly half of its land area reclaimed from the sea, and much of its "nether lands" still below sea level. While the Dutch have had an endless struggle with floods since ancient times, they have valiantly won the battle with them by building dikes and windmills, and reclaiming land areas called *polders*.

One of my memorable journeys in Holland was to follow the final seventy-five-mile stretch of the Rhine that forms its delta. Once the great river entered the North Sea near The Hague where there is still an unimportant waterway called the Old Rhine. But its course has since shifted to the south. At present the Rhine divides, near the German-Dutch border, into two tributaries.

The northern channel, known as the Lek, flows past Arnhem and Rotterdam to reach the North Sea at the Hook of Holland. The southern channel, known as the Waal, is larger. It flows past Nijmegen into the great estuary of the Hollandseh Diep, which it shares with its neighbor, the Maas (Meuse) River. Canals link the southern channel with Rotterdam.

The area known as the Delta covers part of South Holland and Zeeland. Here are the great rivers mentioned above: the Rhine, the Waal, the Maas, and the Schelde. It's a land of considerable contrasts, ranging from the country's richest and most influential province, to charming, beautiful seaside landscapes with islands and semi-islands linked by dikes. Middleburg, Zeeland's largest town at Holland's isolated southwest tip, was once an important trading center and still has street names called Beer Dock and Grain Dock as well as a thriving Thursday market. The town also has a diverse assortment of cafés and restaurants offering exceptional local Dutch dishes, especially fish and shellfish. Zeeland, or Sea Land, has a bounty of herring, oysters, turbot, sole, and smoked fish.

The Dutch are hearty eaters, and they take their food seriously, frequently, and in quantity. At home there are usually five daily repasts, beginning with a substantial breakfast of meat and cheese slices, eggs, breads, butter, jam, and coffee or tea.

The Dutch have high-quality food products and prefer to eat them simply and freshly cooked. Besides its variety of fish and seafood, Holland has many kinds of fruits and vegetables, for the reclaimed *polder* land is notoriously productive. All towns have marvelous markets and shops filled with an amazing variety of all kinds of appealing foods.

In Holland, palates are pampered, but substance is favored over subtlety. The Dutch delight in food fit to sink the teeth into—hearty soups and thick stews, pork, sausage, potatoes, cabbage, robust breads, substantial desserts, and internationally known cheeses. Bordered by the North Sea and traversed by numerous rivers, estuaries, and channels, the country has built its prosperity upon maritime trade. Since their golden age of the 1600s, a time of world-wide commerce and fabulous wealth when the tiny nation ruled a vast empire of what were once called "the spice islands," the Dutch have prized the delicacies of faraway places. Thanks to their adventurous mariners and colonists, the people developed a passion for ginger, cinnamon, and nutmeg, and the cooking is also spiced with the exotic flavors of the East Indies. Curries, Indonesian dishes such as *nasi goreng* and *saté*, and the remarkable institution known as the *rijsttafel* (rice table) have found a second home in Holland.

Another national favorite, chocolate, reached Holland via Spain from the New World and is relished in delightful desserts and candies that are displayed attractively in alluring chocolate shops. It was the founder of a Dutch company, C.J. Van Houten who in 1898 invented the cocoa press that removed most of the cocoa butter from chocolate, thus creating chocolate powder, or cocoa, and a new beverage. Coffee from the Indonesian island of Java (which was nicknamed for it) is drunk in great quantities. Because France under Napoleon dominated Holland from 1795 to 1815, the French cuisine has been highly favored with a direct influence on the sauces, pastries and desserts.

From the Dutch the world acquired many culinary gifts, including gin, palatable liqueurs, and the incomparable Hollandaise sauce. Although it was the French who thickened and perfected it by adding egg yolks, it had its genesis in *beurre Hollandaise*, a simple melted butter sauce for fish.

One of the best places to enjoy and explore Holland's culinary treats is in Rotterdam, the country's second largest city and the world's largest harbor, situated in a strategic position on the delta of the Rhine and Maas rivers. The multicultural city is sometimes called the "Wonder" or "Destroyed" City, because it was virtually flattened by bombs during World War II and was rebuilt from the ground up. From here one can take waterway excursions and visit all kinds of eating places, from the museum and trendy cafés to hotel dining rooms.

The one thing I've always found in Holland, from paintings exalting the humble potato and women preparing enormous meals, to spice shops selling glorious dried fruits and nuts, and bakeries proffering sugary doughnuts called *oliebollen*, is the Dutch passion for good eating and dining. Today this continues as it has for centuries. This selection of recipes gives you the opportunity to experience some of the traditional cookery.

DUTCH CHEESES

One of the joys of visiting Holland is to taste the local cheeses and cheese dishes. Nature provided the country with the perfect blend of climate and fertile flat lands for lush pastures where prized herds are pampered and graze on special grasses and herbs so that their creamy rich milk is extra flavorful. Dutch farmers have long used their bounty to make wholesome cheeses, and their products have been highly prized in European markets since the twelfth century. Pilgrims carried Dutch cheeses on the Mayflower en route to America.

The three best-known cheeses are named after the towns where they were originally made. Edam, from North Holland, is a semisoft orange-yellow cheese with a mild, nutlike flavor. Gouda, from South Holland, is similar to Edam in flavor and texture but is slightly tangier, light yellow, and has a flattened top and bottom. When sold domestically both cheeses are yellow. The familiar waxy-red jackets are added to those shipped abroad. Each should be well aged to develop a full-bodied quality. Leyden, named for the university town called Leiden, is a firm, light yellow cheese that comes in two kinds made tangy with either caraway or cumin seeds.

Lesser known but flavorful cheeses are the rich, nutty Kernhem, good with fruit; a farmer's cheese called Boerenkaas, round and flat topped with an intense flavor; clove-flavored Friesian; Texelaar, creamy and soft and coated with yellow wax; and Maasdammer and Aalsdammer, Swiss-style cheeses.

Cheese plays an important role in the life of everyone in Holland. It's eaten at nearly every meal, including breakfast. Cheeses go well with the creamy butter and all kinds of nutritious white and dark breads. Various types of cheese are sold in shops thinly sliced or in one piece, either as snacks to be eaten on the premises or to take out. In *brodjeswenkels* (delicatessens) one dines on cheeses with hot rolls, condiments, and heavy Dutch beer. Cheese, or cheese sticks, balls, or truffles are enjoyed as appetizers with genever (Dutch gin), the traditional drink.

Dutch cooks also make flavorful cheese sandwiches, soups, souf-flés, croquettes, casseroles, puffs, pies, sauces, and vegetable dishes. Given below are recipes for some Dutch cheese specialties.

Gouda festival.

APPETIZERS

In Holland, eating goes on all day so it is sometimes difficult to distinguish appetizers from snacks, but certainly smoked fish, herring, Zeeland oysters, plovers' eggs, and cheese preparations, served with chilled *genever* or beer, rate highly with the Dutch.

CHEESE TRUFFLES

These little appetizers called *kaastruffels* are made with three favorite Dutch foods: cheese, butter, and pumpernickel. Either the round, crimson-coated Edam or the yellow Gouda may be used. Both are mild, firm, and similar in flavor.

½ cup (1 stick) unsalted butter, softened
¼ pound grated Gouda or Edam cheese
¼ teaspoon paprika
⅛ teaspoon freshly grated nutmeg
Salt, freshly ground pepper
3 to 4 slices pumpernickel, toasted twice

In a medium bowl combine the butter, cheese, paprika, and nutmeg. Season with salt and pepper. Refrigerate, covered, 20 minutes. Shape into small balls. Refrigerate for 20 minutes. Whirl toast in a blender or crush with a rolling pin to make crumbs. Roll each cheese ball in the crumbs. Refrigerate, covered with plastic wrap, 1 hour, up to 6. Makes about 20.

DUTCH HERRING

The humble salt herring, *haring*, caught in large quantities in the North Sea, has been a Dutch staple for centuries, treasured for its high protein and low cost. Over the years, when food was scarce, herring prevented starvation. The Dutch became the envy and enemy of all their neighbors for their domination of the herring interests; because of this their vast foreign fleet was built. Northern towns were created because of the fish. In fact, one adage has it that "the foundations of Amsterdam were laid on herring bones."

The herring is still so popular and important in Holland that the arrival of the first of the season's catch, the *groene haring*, green herring, is a widely heralded national event. In coastal villages it is great fun to watch the expertise of the Dutch in handling a snack of raw herring. Held by the tail, the fish is dipped in raw onion and then nibbled, leaving only the framework of bones. Passersby often stop at street-side pushcarts or open-air stands for a snack of raw herring and chopped onion. Various dishes, including this appetizer, feature the favorite fish.

Serve chilled bite-size pieces of pickled herring, garnished with chopped fresh parsley, onion and tomato slices, with toast and sweet butter. Serve with cool beer.

ARNHEM BITTERBALLEN

Arnhem, once a wealthy resort in the province of Gelderland and almost totally destroyed in World War II, is now a lively capital city. Immortalized in the book and film, *A Bridge Too Far*, Arnhem is a convenient center for sightseeing at nearby attractions including the Netherlands Open Air Museum, founded in 1912 to preserve the country's architectural and cultural heritage, and the wartime sites of Operation Market. There also is a wide range of good eating places to enjoy local drinks and appetizers.

These savory meatballs, actually a type of croquette, are favorite Dutch appetizers. The name, *bitterballen*, is said to derive from "bitters," as the appetizers are served with drinks, especially gin and bitters.

¼ cup (½ stick) unsalted butter, cut up
¼ cup all-purpose flour
1 cup beef bouillon
1 teaspoon Worcestershire sauce
⅛ teaspoon freshly grated nutmeg
3 tablespoons finely chopped onion
2 tablespoons chopped fresh parsley
1½ cups finely chopped cooked meat (beef or veal)
Salt, freshly ground pepper
Fine dry bread crumbs
2 eggs, beaten
Fat for deep-frying

In a medium saucepan melt butter over medium-high heat. Stir in flour; blend well. Add bouillon, ⅓ cup at a time, stirring after each addition. Cook, stirring, until sauce is thickened and smooth. Add Worcestershire, nutmeg, onion, parsley and chopped meat. Season with salt and pepper. Mix well. Reduce heat to medium-low. Cook, stirring, to prevent mixture from sticking to the pan, about 15 minutes. Remove from the heat.

Spoon into a buttered pie plate or shallow dish, spreading evenly. Refrigerate, covered with plastic wrap, until set, about 2 hours. Shape into small bite-size balls. Roll in bread crumbs, then in beaten egg, and again in bread crumbs. Refrigerate, covered with plastic wrap, 1 hour, up to 6. Fry in hot fat (390 degrees) until golden brown. Drain on paper towels. Serve at once with sharp mustard. Makes about 35.

UITSMIJTER

The popular open-faced sandwich called *uitsmijter* (pronounced out-smay-ter), translated as "throw out" or "bouncer," is so named because it was the custom to have the sandwich as a late evening snack just before a restaurant closed its doors. Sold at eating places throughout the country, the popular sandwich comes in three types: roast beef, ham, or veal. It's easy to prepare in the home.

Place several thin slices of cold cooked ham or beef on a slice of buttered plain or toasted white bread and top with one or two fried eggs. Garnish with a dill-pickle fan or gherkin.

SPLIT GREEN PEA SOUP

The national soup of Holland, *Erwtensoep*, green pea soup, is made in many varieties that are served throughout the country as a winter staple. Each cook has a favorite recipe that generally includes green split peas, pork, and vegetables. Properly prepared, the hearty one-dish meal should be so thick that a spoon can stand upright in the rich purée. It is best cooked the day beforehand, left overnight, and then reheated. A good accompaniment is pumpernickel. This is a traditional version of the soup.

2 cups (1 pound) split green peas, washed and picked over
3 quarts water
Salt
2 large pigs' feet, cleaned and split
1 pound smoked bacon or pork in one piece
2 medium leeks, white parts and 2 inches green, cleaned
    and sliced thickly
4 medium potatoes, pared and diced
1 small celeriac (celery root), peeled and diced
Freshly ground pepper
½ pound frankfurters, sliced into ½-inch rounds

In a pot combine the green peas and water. Season with salt. Bring to a boil over medium-high heat. Reduce heat to medium-low. Cook, covered, for 1 hour. Add pigs' feet and bacon. Continue to cook for another 40 minutes. Add leeks, potatoes, celeriac, and pepper. Continue to cook another 30 minutes. Remove from heat. Take out bacon and pigs' feet. Cut any meat from the feet, discarding the bones and skin. Cut bacon into slices. Return meat and bacon to the pot. Add frankfurter slices. Check the seasoning. Reheat over low heat or leave overnight and reheat the next day. Serve in soup plates. 8 servings.

MAASTRICHT CHEESE SOUP

Maastricht, capital of the Limburg province in the far south-eastern corner of Holland, is a cosmopolitan city with a rich history dating back to the time of the Romans when legions were searching for a place to bridge the Rhine. Now a harmonious blend of the past and present, it is best known as the symbol of the European Union since the signing of the Maastricht Treaty in 1992, the first agreement to political, economic, and monetary union. It also has been called Holland's gastronomic capital, noted for its fine cooking and specialties such as white asparagus, fresh-water trout, and fruit tarts.

This cheese soup, *kaas soep*, is named for the charming city.

4 slices thin bacon, diced
¼ cup (½ stick) unsalted butter
1 medium yellow onion, peeled and finely chopped
2 tablespoons tomato paste
1 teaspoon Dijon-style mustard
1 teaspoon Worcestershire sauce
⅛ teaspoon paprika
Salt, freshly ground pepper
4 cups rich chicken broth
2 cups shredded Edam cheese
2 cups hot light cream or milk
Croutons (optional)

In a large saucepan cook the bacon over medium-high heat until crisp. Pour off the fat. Add butter and melt. Add chopped onion; sauté until translucent, about 5 minutes. Add tomato paste, mustard, Worcestershire, and paprika. Season with salt and pepper. Mix well. Cook 1 or 2 minutes, stirring, to blend flavors. Pour in chicken broth. Bring soup to a boil. Reduce heat to medium-low. Cook, covered, for 30 minutes. Add cheese; continue to cook over low heat until melted. Pour in cream or milk; mix well. Leave on stove long enough to heat. Serve with croutons, if desired. 8 servings.

CURRY SOUP WITH BEANS

Another traditional soup, called *kerriesoep met bonen,* is a good winter supper dish.

2 cups (1 pound) dried lima beans, washed and picked over
4 whole cloves
4 whole peppercorns
1 bay leaf
½ teaspoon chili powder
2 medium yellow onions, peeled and chopped
1 cup sliced scraped carrots
1 leek, white part only, cleaned and sliced thinly
3 tablespoons unsalted butter
2 tablespoons curry powder
½ teaspoon paprika

In a pot soak the beans in 10 cups of water according to package directions. Add cloves, peppercorns, bay leaf, and chili powder. Bring to a boil over medium-high heat. Reduce heat to medium-low. Cook, covered, stirring occasionally, for 1½ hours. Add onions, carrots, and leek. Continue to cook until beans and vegetables are tender, about 45 minutes. Remove from heat. Cool. Remove and discard cloves, peppercorns, and bay leaf. Purée in a food processor or blender. Reheat.

Meanwhile, in a small skillet melt butter over medium-high heat. Add curry powder and paprika. Cook a few seconds. Stir into hot soup. 10 to 12 servings.

SCALLOPED EGGS WITH CHEESE

This appealing typical dish, made with Holland's great Gouda cheese, can be served as a first course or a luncheon specialty.

4 large eggs
2 slices thin bacon, minced
About 3 tablespoons unsalted butter
1 medium yellow onion, peeled and finely chopped
4 medium tomatoes, peeled and finely chopped
Salt, freshly ground pepper
2 tablespoons all-purpose flour
1 cup light cream or milk
½ cup grated Gouda cheese
Fine dry bread crumbs
Paprika

Preheat broiler. Hard-cook eggs; shell them. Set aside.

In a medium skillet combine minced bacon and 1 tablespoon butter. Fry bacon over medium-high heat until crisp. Add onion; sauté until translucent, about 5 minutes. Mix in chopped tomatoes. Season with salt and pepper. Cook slowly 5 minutes. Remove from stove; set aside.

In a small saucepan melt 1 tablespoon butter over medium-high heat. Stir in flour. Cook l minute. Gradually add cream or milk. Cook, stirring, until thickened and smooth. Stir in ⅓ cup cheese and a little paprika. Season with salt and pepper. Reduce heat to medium-low. Cook until cheese melts. Remove from stove.

Place each of the cooked eggs in a scallop shell or ramekin. Spoon onion-tomato mixture around the eggs, dividing evenly. Spoon cheese sauce over and around the eggs. Sprinkle with dry bread crumbs, the remaining 3 tablespoons of cheese, and a little paprika. Dot the tops with bits of butter. Put under broiler until hot and bubbly, about 5 minutes. 4 servings.

DORDRECHT SHRIMP CROQUETTES

Once the wealthiest trading town and port in Holland, Dordrecht sits picturesquely between two branches of the Rhine. During the seventeenth and eighteenth centuries it was an inspiration for Dutch painters. The old town is divided by three waterways, including the main canal that winds through the town's center, flowing beside the *Voorstraat*, the primary shopping street lined with handsome houses, tiny shops, and restaurants. North of the city are the famous windmills of Kinderdijk, the largest collection of originals with 19 of them built between 1722 and 1761.

In Holland the shrimp, or *garnalen*, are very tiny and time-consuming to shell and clean. They are treasured, however, for their delicate flavor. This typical dish can be served as a luncheon or supper entrée.

3 tablespoons unsalted butter
¼ cup all-purpose flour
1 cup light cream
⅛ teaspoon freshly grated nutmeg
Salt, freshly ground pepper
2 large eggs
2 cups chopped, cleaned, cooked small shrimp
2 tablespoons chopped fresh parsley
Juice of 1 lemon
Fine dry bread crumbs
Fat for deep-frying

In a medium saucepan melt butter over medium-high heat. Stir in flour. Cook, stirring, 1 minute. Gradually add cream. Reduce heat to medium-low. Cook, stirring, until thickened and smooth. Add nutmeg. Season with salt and pepper.

Meanwhile, separate 1 egg. In a small dish beat the egg yolk with a fork; mix in some of the hot sauce. Return to the rest of the sauce. Add shrimp, parsley, and lemon juice. Mix well. Remove from stove. In a medium bowl beat egg white until stiff. Fold carefully into shrimp mixture. Spoon into a flat dish, spreading evenly; cool. Divide mixture into 12 equal parts. Form each part into a 2-inch ball. Refrigerate, covered with plastic wrap, for 1 hour. In a shallow dish beat the remaining egg lightly. Roll each croquette in bread crumbs, then in beaten egg, and again in bread crumbs. Refrigerate, covered with plastic wrap, for 1 hour, up to 6. Fry in hot fat (390 degrees) until golden. Drain on paper towels. 4 to 6 servings.

HUSSARS' SALAD

The name for this hearty salad originated in the small Dutch garrisons where the *hussars* (mounted soldiers) were stationed and often dined with the local families who made dishes with leftovers for them. Serve this combination salad for an informal winter meal.

2 cups diced cold, cooked beef, veal, or pork
2 cups diced cold, cooked potatoes
1 cup cold, cooked green peas
1 medium yellow onion, peeled and diced
2 tablespoons sweet relish
2 hard-cooked eggs, shelled and chopped
1 medium tart apple, cored and diced
¼ cup olive or vegetable oil
2 tablespoons wine vinegar
1½ tablespoons chopped fresh dill or ½ teaspoon dried dillweed
Salt, freshly ground pepper
Crisp lettuce leaves, washed and dried
About ¾ cup mayonnaise
1 medium tomato, peeled and sliced
3 tablespoons chopped fresh parsley

In a large bowl combine diced meat, potatoes, peas, onion, relish, eggs, and apples. In a small dish combine oil, vinegar, and dill or dillweed. Add to meat-vegetable mixture. Season with salt and pepper. Refrigerate, covered, 2 hours, up to 6, to blend flavors. When ready to serve, arrange lettuce leaves on a serving dish. Top with the salad, shaping into a mound. Cover with a thin coating of mayonnaise. Garnish with sliced tomatoes and parsley. 4 to 6 servings.

HUTSPOT

*H*utspot, a Dutch word meaning "hodge-podge" or "hot pot", is a beloved family dish comprising a purée of vegetables and various cuts of beef. It is eaten annually on October 3 to celebrate the end of the lengthy Spanish siege of Leiden in 1574. When hope of the starving people was lowest, the Dutch fleet came to the rescue and supposedly brought pots of *hutspot* with them. Thus the grateful Dutch make this stew as a traditional dish for their Thanksgiving feast.

2 pounds beef chuck or flank
4 cups water
1 teaspoon salt
1½ pounds carrots, scraped and sliced
2 pounds (about 6 medium) potatoes, peeled and quartered
2 large yellow onions, peeled and chopped
2 tablespoons light cream or milk
2 tablespoons unsalted butter
Freshly ground pepper

Cut any fat from the chuck or flank and, if the flank is used, take off any membranes. Put in a large saucepan with the water and salt. Bring to a boil over medium- high heat. Remove any scum that rises to the top. Reduce heat to medium-low. Cook, covered, 1 hour. Add carrots, potatoes, and onions. Continue cooking until the vegetables are tender, about 40 minutes. Remove meat to a warm platter; cut into strips. If flank is used, it should be cut against the grain. Remove vegetables to a bowl. Add cream or milk and butter. Season with salt and pepper. Mash or purée, adding some of the broth to thin the mixture, if desired. To serve, spoon the vegetables onto a platter and surround with the meat slices. 4 to 6 servings.

NIJMEGEN PORK CHOPS WITH APPLES

Nijmegen, situated on the southern bank of the Waal River, just to the west of its junction with the Rhine, has long been strategically important because of its location. It was an imperial city of the Hanseatic Empire and a principal seat of the Holy Roman Emperor Charlemagne. In World War II, however, much of the Old Town was largely destroyed but there are still several historical buildings and museums. The city now attracts Rhine sightseers and is a center for river excursions.

The Dutch are fond of hearty dishes combining meats, especially pork, with fruit. This specialty is one of the best.

2 pounds (about 6 medium) potatoes, peeled and cubed
6 tart apples, peeled, cored, and chopped
2 medium yellow onions, peeled and chopped
2 cups beef bouillon
1 teaspoon ground cinnamon
Salt, freshly ground pepper
6 center-cut loin pork chops
2 tablespoons chopped fresh parsley
12 fresh pork sausage links, cooked and drained

In a large saucepan combine potatoes, apples, onions, bouillon, and cinnamon. Season with salt and pepper. Bring to a boil over medium-high heat. Reduce the heat to medium-low. Cook, covered, until potatoes are tender and most of the liquid has been absorbed, about 25 minutes. Remove from the stove; keep warm.

Meanwhile, cut any excess fat from the pork chops. In a medium skillet melt 1 piece of the fat over medium-high heat. Add pork chops and brown on both sides. Season with salt and pepper. Add ¼ cup water. Reduce heat to medium-low. Cook, covered, until chops are well done, about 30 minutes. Remove to drain on paper towels.

To serve, spoon hot potato and apple mixture into a mound in the center of a platter. Sprinkle with parsley. Arrange cooked pork chops and sausages around the potato mixture. Serve at once. 6 servings.

Traditional dress.

INDONESIAN BAHMI GORENG

The Dutch cuisine is spiced with exotic flavors from the East Indies, particularly foods and dishes from Indonesia. One of the most popular is *bahmi goreng*, made with noodles.

½ pound fine egg noodles or vermicelli
1½ pounds boneless pork strips, without fat
½ cup soy sauce
2 garlic cloves, crushed
6 scallions, with some tops, finely chopped
About ½ cup peanut oil
2 eggs, beaten
2 large yellow onions, peeled and thinly sliced
2 teaspoons minced gingerroot
1 cup drained bean sprouts
3 cups chopped Chinese cabbage
1½ cups cleaned, shelled, cooked small or medium shrimp
Freshly ground black pepper

In a large saucepan cook noodles in boiling salted water according to package directions until tender. Drain and spread out on a large plate; cool. Refrigerate, covered with plastic wrap, 2 hours.

In a large bowl combine pork strips, ⅓ cup soy sauce, garlic, and scallions. Mix well. Marinate, stirring occasionally, for 2 hours.

In a medium skillet heat a little oil over medium-low heat. Add beaten eggs; tilt at once to spread evenly. Cook until set. Remove to a plate and cool. Cut into strips. Set aside to use as a garnish.

When ready to cook, in a large skillet heat 2 tablespoons oil over medium-high heat. Add pork mixture. Sauté until pork is cooked. Remove to a plate. Heat 2 tablespoons oil in the skillet. Add onions and gingerroot. Sauté until translucent, about 5 minutes. Remove to a plate. Heat 3 tablespoons oil; sauté the bean sprouts, Chinese cabbage, and shrimp. Sauté 5 minutes. Return the cooked pork, onions, and gingerroot to the mixture. Stir in remaining 3 tablespoons soy sauce. Season with pepper. Leave over low heat.

In another skillet heat 3 tablespoons oil over medium-high heat. Add cold noodles. Cook until golden and crisp. With a slotted spoon remove to the pork-shrimp mixture. Serve on a platter garnished with the cooked egg strips. 4 to 6 servings.

LIMBURG BEEF STEW

This hearty beef stew called *haché* is named for Limburg, Holland's southernmost province that is a finger of land between Belgium and Germany. Here farming is an important occupation.

6 tablespoons unsalted butter
3 large yellow onions, peeled and chopped
2 tablespoons all-purpose flour
2 cups beef bouillon
2 bay leaves
4 whole cloves
Salt, freshly ground pepper
2 pounds round steak, cut into 1-inch cubes
2 tablespoons wine vinegar
1 tablespoon Worcestershire sauce

In a large saucepan melt 3 tablespoons butter over medium-high heat. Add chopped onions; sauté until translucent, about 5 minutes. Stir in flour; blend well. Add beef bouillon; cook, stirring, until thickened and smooth. Add bay leaves and cloves. Season with salt and pepper. Reduce heat to medium-low. Cook, covered, 5 minutes.

Meanwhile, in a medium skillet melt remaining 3 tablespoons butter over medium-high heat. Add steak cubes; brown on all sides. Add, with vinegar, to the sauce. Continue cooking, covered, until meat is tender, stirring occasionally, about 40 minutes. Add Worcestershire just before serving. Remove and discard bay leaves and cloves. Serve with boiled potatoes and red cabbage. 6 servings.

KALE WITH POTATOES

The Dutch are devotees of a country dish called *stamppot*, a name that derives from the thorough mixing together of the ingredients such as two or three kinds of vegetables. They are sometimes served with sausages or pork on top.

2 large potatoes, peeled and quartered
2 tablespoons bacon fat or unsalted butter
1 package (10 ounces) frozen chopped kale
2 tablespoons light cream
Salt, freshly ground pepper

In a medium saucepan boil potatoes in salted water over medium-high heat until tender, about 15 minutes. Drain and turn into a large bowl. Add bacon fat or butter; mash to purée. Meanwhile, cook chopped kale until tender; drain. Add cream; mix well. Add to hot potato mixture. Mash to blend well. Season with salt and pepper. 4 to 6 servings.

BEETS WITH APPLES

This is a good accompaniment for meat or game.

1 can (1 pound) or 2 cups sliced beets, drained
1 cup chopped onions
3 medium tart apples, peeled, cored, and chopped
2 teaspoons sugar
2 tablespoons unsalted butter
⅛ teaspoon freshly grated nutmeg
Salt, freshly ground pepper
3 tablespoons wine vinegar

In a medium saucepan combine beets, onions, apples, sugar, butter, and nutmeg over medium-low heat. Season with salt and pepper. Cook, covered, until mixture is a purée, about 45 minutes. Add vinegar; stir. Remove from heat; mash. 4 to 6 servings.

CHEESE SAUCE

Serve with hard-cooked eggs, pasta, or vegetables.

3 tablespoons unsalted butter
3 tablespoons all-purpose flour
1½ cups light cream or milk
1 cup grated Gouda or Edam cheese
1 teaspoon prepared mustard
⅛ teaspoon paprika
Salt, freshly ground pepper

In a medium saucepan melt butter over medium-high heat. Add flour; mix well. Gradually add cream or milk, stirring while adding. Cook until thickened and smooth. Stir in cheese. Add mustard and paprika. Season with salt and pepper. Cook until cheese melts, about 8 minutes. Makes about 2 cups.

APPLE FRITTERS

Apples have long flourished in Holland's mildly cold, damp climate and are noted for their delicious flavor and color. Dutch cooks prepare excellent apple cakes, apple balls wrapped in pastry and baked, and simple but delectable puddings made of layers of applesauce and buttered bread slices. Another treasured specialty is apple fritters, *appelbeignets,* made by dipping slices of cored, peeled apples in a beer batter and frying them in hot deep fat or oil. Stacks of the fritters, sprinkled with confectioners' sugar, are prepared annually in Dutch homes to serve children at the traditional Saint Nicholas Day celebration on December 6.

1 cup all-purpose flour
½ teaspoon salt
1 cup light beer, at room temperature
4 medium tart apples
¾ cup sugar
½ teaspoon ground cinnamon
Vegetable oil for deep-frying
Confectioners' sugar

Into a medium bowl sift the flour and salt. Make a well in the center. Slowly add the beer, stirring to make a smooth, thick batter. Do not beat. Set aside to remain at room temperature for 2 hours before frying.

About 15 minutes before making the fritters, peel and core apples. Cut crosswise into ¼-inch rounds. Place apple rounds on a sheet of wax paper. In a small dish combine sugar and cinnamon. Sprinkle over both sides of each apple round.

Preheat oven to 275 degrees. In a deep-fryer heat add vegetable oil to a depth of about 3 inches. Heat to 375 degrees. With tongs dip each apple slice into the batter. Fry a few at a time until golden and puffed, about 4 minutes. As they are cooked, keep warm in the oven.

To serve, arrange on a platter. Sprinkle with confectioners' sugar. Makes about 16.

PANCAKES

One of the traditional dishes of Holland is pancakes, *pannekoeken*, that are made in fascinating variety. Simple to prepare with a few ingredients, inexpensive, and nourishing, they have long been made for breakfast, lunch, and supper as well as family and holiday celebrations. The pancakes can be small, medium, or very large, up to 12 to 15 inches across, and served plain or with fillings and toppings. Throughout the country itinerant vendors make and serve pancakes and the whole nation seems to relish them wherever they happen to be, at fairs and carnivals, the beach or on the tables of restaurants called *pannekoekenhuysje*, pancake houses. There is also a dessert pancake, *poffertje*, small and often including fruit, liqueurs, and chocolate that is sometimes served with a sweet topping.

Thin pancakes, *flensjes*, are simply made with a thin batter of flour, eggs, and milk, and fried in butter. They may be small or medium and are served flat, in layers, and with a filling of custard sauce in between each layer, or rolled up. A cake called *flensjes* is composed of a stack of about seven pancakes, spread only with applesauce, or also with fruit purée, and served in pie-shaped wedges. Here's a recipe for this variety.

¾ cup all-purpose flour
3 large eggs
Salt
2 cups milk
Unsalted butter
Confectioners' sugar
Currant jelly

Put flour in a large bowl. Make a well in the center. In a small dish whisk eggs and salt until light and fluffy. Pour into the well. Mix to combine well. Add milk, ½ cup at a time; mix well. Whisk until batter is smooth and thin. Lightly butter a 6- or 7-inch skillet over medium-high heat. Pour in 2 tablespoons of the batter. Tilt the pan at once so the entire surface is coated. Cook until edges shrink from sides of the pan. Remove the pancake by inverting it onto a plate. Sprinkle lightly with confectioners' sugar. Place a spoonful of jelly along the center and roll up. Keep warm until all pancakes are cooked. Serve immediately. Makes about 24 pancakes.

THE HAGUE BLUFF

This favorite dessert of Dutch children is named bluff because it is made out of a very little but looks like a great deal. Contrary to what many people believe, The Hague that the Dutch call *Den Haag*, is not Holland's capital. It is Amsterdam.

1 egg white
½ cup sugar
3 tablespoons red currant or raspberry syrup

In a large bowl beat the egg white until fluffy. Add sugar and syrup, a little at a time, and continue beating until light and fluffy. Spoon into dessert dishes. Serve with cookies. 4 servings.

LEMON CREAM

This wine-flavored cream dessert is called *Citroenvla*. It's pleasing and light, and easy to prepare.

4 large eggs, separated
½ cup sugar
½ cup dry white wine
Juice of 2 lemons
Grated rind of ½ lemon

In the top of a double boiler beat egg yolks with the sugar. Add wine, lemon juice, and rind. Cook over hot simmering water, not boiling, beating vigorously, until mixture thickens. Remove from the stove and cool.

Meanwhile, in a large bowl beat egg whites until stiff but not dry. Fold into cooled wine mixture. Spoon into serving dishes. Garnish with whole strawberries, if desired. 4 servings.

EGGNOG

A popular Dutch drink called *Advocaat*, made with eggs, sugar, and brandy, is sometimes called eggnog. It's also eaten as a dessert.

6 large eggs
1 cup sugar
1½ cups brandy
1 teaspoon vanilla
Garnishes: Sweetened whipped cream, freshly grated nutmeg

In a large bowl whisk eggs until frothy. Beat in sugar, a little at a time, until light. Transfer mixture to the top of a double boiler set over hot but not boiling water over medium heat. Add the brandy and vanilla in a steady stream, beating with a whisk, until thick and frothy. Remove from the heat. Whisk egg-sugar mixture until it is lukewarm. Spoon, dividing equally, into 6 sherbet or dessert glasses. Cool slightly. Serve garnished with whipped cream and nutmeg. 6 servings.

DUTCH DRINKS

Although Holland grows no wine grapes, it is one of the great drink-producing countries of the world, known for a number of outstanding drinks.

The indigenous drink is *genever* (aka *jenever*), Dutch gin, a colorless, volatile, aromatic, and slightly bitter spirit. Created by a chemist, Franz de le Boe, also known as Dr. Sylvius, it was distilled from grain into a medicinal beverage that he flavored with juniper berries and called *jenever* after the French word for juniper, *genièvre*. First sold in apothecaries it proved to be so popular that distilleries began making and selling the drink. Later, when introduced into England the name was shortened to gin.

Genever, however, is quite different from what the world knows as gin. Because of its pronounced flavor, it is served, slightly chilled, in small glasses, traditionally drunk straight, often in one gulp, as an aperitif before meals, as a digestive afterward, or as a nightcap. It is not suitable for making mixed drinks or cocktails. There are two types, "old" and "new" but the difference between them is not in age. *Oud* (old) *genever* is light yellow and has a rather strong taste and aroma. *Jong* (young) *genever* is white and has a neutral taste. There are also lemon flavored and red currant flavored *genevers*.

After unfavorable wine-import regularities were imposed in Holland, the Dutch created a number of distilled wine drinks including one called *brandewijn*, "burned wine," which the world would know as brandy. In Holland there are many brandy flavors and uses. Drinks combining it with raisins, called "farm boys," or, with apricots, called "farm girls," were once traditional Dutch party drinks.

Dutch distillers also created one of the world's greatest liqueurs, Curaçao, named after the West Indies island from where they imported dried bitter-orange peel that provided essential oils and the fine sweet flavor. It became so popular that many distillers sell it under different names. A liqueur called Triple Sec was originally white Curaçao. Another Dutch creation is a sweet liqueur called Crème de

Cacao, made from cocoa beans imported from the Netherlands Antilles.

In Holland most drinking is done in the cozy surroundings of a brown café (*bruin kroeg*), named for its wooden furnishings and wood-paneled walls mellowed to a golden hue by centuries of tobacco smoke. Very much like a pub, the congenial café is known for its good food, good drink, and good company. Although no longer common, the favorite drinking place once was a *proeflokaal*, or tasting house, used by distillers to introduce the public to their drinks. Virtually every distillery had its own house where potential customers could sample a few liqueurs and then place their orders. Essentially, however, the houses were stores rather than bars. They had no tables or chairs and closed early. Today there are still a few of the restored traditional Dutch tasting houses that are set up as bars and sell food and drinks. The colorful names range from Three Bottles and Little Doctor to The Admiral. Many of them are known also for their antique furnishings and collections of bottles and artifacts.

In Holland beer is the everyday drink with Heineken and Amstel the best known of the brews.

BIBLIOGRAPHY

Baedeker, Karl. *Baedeker's Frankfurt.* Frankfurt: Karl Baedeker, 1960.

Beer, Gretel. *Exploring Rural Austria.* Chicago: Passport Books, 1990.

Fitzgibbon, Theodora. *The Food Of The Western World.* New York: Quadrangle, 1976.

Fodor, Eugene. *Fodor's Guide To Europe.* The Hague: Morton & Co., 1965.

Fodor's Europe. New York: Fodor's Travel Productions, 1997.

Mackenzie, Paul. *Romans On The Rhine.* New York: Funk & Wagnalls, 1970.

Nelson, Kay Shaw. *The Best of Western European Cooking.* New York: John Day, 1976.

————. *The Eastern European Cookbook.* Chicago: Henry Regnery, 1973.

Ogrizek, Dore and Rufenacht, J.G. *Switzerland.* New York: McGraw Hill, 1949.

Root, Waverly. *The Food of France.* New York: Alfred A. Knopf, 1958.

Twain, Mark (Samuel L. Clemens). *A Tramp Abroad.* Hartford: American Publishing Co., 1880.

RECIPE INDEX

SUBJECT INDEX

Also by Kay Shaw Nelson . . .

The Scottish-Irish Pub & Hearth Cookbook

From hearty, wholesome recipes for family dinners, to more sophisticated and exotic dishes for entertaining with flair, this book is the perfect source for dining the Celtic way! In this collection of 170 recipes of the best of Scottish and Irish pub fare and home cooking, you'll find old classics like Corn Beef 'N Cabbage, Cock-A-Leekie, Avalon Apple Pie, and Fish and Chips, and new recipes as well: Tobermory Smoked Salmon Pâté, Raisin Walnut Porridge, and Skibbereen Scallop-Mushroom Pie. Each chapter begins with entertaining stories, legends, and lore about Celtic peoples, traditions, customs, and history.

260 pages • 5½ x 8½ • b/w photos/illustrations • 0-7818-0741-7 • $24.95hc • (164)

Other cookbooks of interest from Hippocrene . . .

All Along the Danube, Expanded Edition

Recipes from Germany, Austria, Czechoslovakia, Yugoslavia, Hungary, Romania, and Bulgaria
Marina Polvay
Now updated with a section on classic Central European wines!

For novices and gourmets, this unique cookbook offers a tempting variety of over 300 Central European recipes from the shores of the Danube River, bringing Old World flavor to today's dishes.

357 pages • 5½ x 8½ • numerous b/w photos & illustrations • 0-7818-0806-5 • $14.95pb • (479)

Bavarian Cooking

Olli Leeb

With over 300 recipes, this lovely collector's item cookbook covers every aspect of Bavarian cuisine from drinks, salads and breads, to main courses and desserts. Some traditional recipes include Suckling Pig, Stuffed Pigeons, Hot Sprout Salad, Mushrooms in Cream Sauce, Toasted Potato Dumplings, and of course, the world-famous Bavarian Cream. Includes charming line drawings, nine color photos, and an illustrated map of Old Bavaria.

176 pages • 6½ x 8¼ • 0-7818-0561-9 • $25.00hc • (659)

Best of Austrian Cuisine

Elisabeth Mayer-Browne

Nearly 200 recipes from Austria's rich cuisine: roasted meats in cream sauces, hearty soups and stews, tasty dumplings, and of course, the pastries and cakes that remain Vienna's trademark.

224 pages • 5 x 8½ • 0-7818-0526-0 • $11.95pb • (633)

The Swiss Cookbook

Nika Standen Hazelton

Drawing from her long experience of and affection for Switzerland, cookbook expert Nika Hazelton explains the basic elements of Swiss cooking as it is practiced in Swiss homes. Her "lessons" include such necessities as complete directions for "au bleu" fish cookery, for making superb dumplings or Swiss pasta, for plain or fancy fondue in all its variations, and for roasting veal in the Swiss manner. The book's 250

recipes, gathered over many years from peasants, housewives, and chefs through history, cover the range of home cooking, from appetizers to desserts, all adapted for the American kitchen.
236 pages • 5½ x 8½ • 0-7818-0587-2 • $11.95pb • (726)

The Art of Dutch Cooking
C. Countess van Limburg Stirum
This attractive volume offers a complete cross section of Dutch home cooking, adapted to American kitchens. A whole chapter is devoted to the Dutch Christmas, with recipes for unique cookies and candies that are a traditional part of the festivities. There are separate chapters on potatoes (a national favorite), on party beverages—including several superb champagne punches—and on Indonesian dishes from the Dutch East Indies. Many of the 200 recipes can be wholly or partially prepared beforehand.
192 pages • 5½ x 8¼ • 0-7818-0582-1 • $11.95pb • (683)

Taste of Romania, Expanded Edition
Nicolae Klepper
Now updated with a chapter of Romanian-Jewish Recipes!
"A brilliant cultural and culinary history . . . a collection of recipes to be treasured, tested and enjoyed."—George Lang, owner of Café des Artistes
" . . . dishes like creamy cauliflower soup, sour cream-enriched *mamaliga* (the Romanian polenta), lamb stewed in sauerkraut juice and scallions, and *mititei* (exactly like the ones I tasted so long ago in Bucharest) are simple and appealing . . . Klepper paints a pretty picture of his native country's culinary possibilities."—Colman Andrews, *Saveur* magazine
A real taste of both Old World and modern Romanian culture. More than 140 recipes, including the specialty dishes of Romania's top chefs, are intermingled with fables, poetry, photos and illustrations in this comprehensive and well-organized guide to Romanian cuisine.
335 pages • 6 x 9 • photos/illustrations • 0-7818-0766-2 • $24.95hc • (462)

Traditional Bulgarian Cooking
Atanas Slavov
This collection of over 125 authentic recipes, the first comprehensive Bulgarian cookbook published in English, spans the range of home cooking: including many stews and hearty soups using lamb or poultry and grilled meats, vegetables and cheese pastries; desserts of sweetmeats rich in sugar and honey, puddings, and dried fruit compotes.
200 pages • 5½ x 8½ • 0-7818-0581-3 • $22.50hc • (681)

The Art of Hungarian Cooking, Revised edition
Paula Pogany Bennett and Velma R. Clark
Whether you crave Chicken Paprika or Apple Strudel, these 222 authentic Hungarian recipes include a vast array of national favorites, from appetizers through desserts. Now updated with a concise guide to Hungarian wines!
225 pages • 5½ x 8½ • 18 b/w drawings • 0-7818-0586-4 • $11.95pb • (686)

Hungarian Cookbook:
Old World Recipes for New World Cooks
Yolanda Nagy Fintor
These Old World recipes were brought to America by the author's grandparents, but they have been updated to accommodate today's faster-paced lifestyle. In many

cases, the author presents a New World version of the recipe, in which low-fat and more readily available ingredients are substituted without compromising flavor. Hungarian cuisine is known for generous amounts of paprika, sour cream, bacon and garlic in famous dishes like "Chicken Paprika" and "Hungarian Goulash." This collection includes these classics, and spans the range of home cooking with recipes for "Bean with Sausage Soup," "Stuffed Breast of Veal," "Hungarian Creamed Spinach," and a host of tempting desserts like "Walnut Torte," and "Dilled Cottage Cheese Cake."

This is more than just a collection of 125 enticing Hungarian recipes. Eight chapters also describe the seasonal and ceremonial holidays that Hungarian-Americans celebrate today with special foods: fall grape festivals; Christmas, New Year's and Easter; summer cookouts; weddings and baptisms. The book also includes culinary tips, a glossary of terms and explanations about the Hungarian language.

190 pages • 5½ x 8½ • $24.95hc • 0-7818-0828-6 • (47)

The Best of Polish Cooking, Expanded Edition
Karen West
Now updated with a new chapter on Light Polish Fare!
"Ethnic cuisine at its best."—*The Midwest Book Review*

First published in 1983, this classic resource for Polish cuisine has been a favorite with home chefs for many years. The new edition includes a chapter on Light Polish Fare with ingenious tips for reducing fat, calories and cholesterol, without compromising the flavor of fine Polish cuisine. Fragrant herbal rubs and vinegars add panache without calories. Alternatives and conversion tables for butter, sour cream and milk will help readers lighten other recipes as well.

In an easy-to-use menu format, the author arranges complementary and harmonious foods together—all organized in seasonal cycles. Inside are recipes for "Braised Spring Lamb with Cabbage," "Frosty Artichoke Salad," "Apple Raisin Cake," and "Hunter's Stew." The new Light Polish Fare chapter includes low-fat recipes for treats like "Roasted Garlic and Mushroom Soup" and "Twelve-Fruit Brandied Compote."

248 pages • 5½ x 8¼ • $9.95pb • 0-7818-0826-X • (274)

Old Polish Traditions in the Kitchen and at the Table
A cookbook and history of Polish culinary customs. Short essays cover subjects like Polish hospitality, holiday traditions, even the exalted status of the mushroom. The recipes are traditional family fare.

304 pages • 6 x 9 • 0-7818-0488-4 • $11.95pb • (546)

The Art of Lithuanian Cooking
Maria Gieysztor de Gorgey
This volume of over 150 authentic Lithuanian recipes includes such classic favorites as Fresh Cucumber Soup, Lithuanian Meat Pockets, Hunter's Stew, Potato Zeppelins, as well as delicacies like Homemade Honey Liqueur and Easter Gypsy Cake. The author's introduction and easy step-by-step instructions ensure that even novice cooks can create authentic, delicious Lithuanian recipes.

230 pages • 5½ x 8½ • 0-7818-0610-7 • $24.95hc • (722)

The Best of Czech Cooking, Expanded Edition
Peter Trnka
Now expanded with 3 new chapters on Pork, Mushrooms, and Drinks, this popular Hippocrene cookbook is better than ever. Czech cuisine emphasizes delicious soups, salads, dumplings, hearty meat dishes, vegetables and desserts, with recipes

that rely on the subtle flavors of fresh ingredients. This new edition includes "Vepro-knedlo-zelo," a classic dish of pork, cabbage and dumplings; an informative chapter about gathering, storing and using wild mushrooms; and a section on aperitifs, wine and beers, including the world-famous Czech Pilsner Urquell beer.
300 pages • 5½ x 8¼ • 0-7818-0805-7 • $24.95hc • (456)

The Best of Slovak Cooking
Sylvia & John Lorinc
   This cookbook features over 100 easy-to-follow Slovak recipes. Along with creative preparation of certain staples such as potatoes, cabbage and noodles, Slovak cuisine is also noted for its pastries, rich butter and cream dishes, and pork specialties. Among the chapters included are: Soups, Vegetables & Side Dishes, Main Dishes, and Desserts & Breads. All recipes are adapted for the North American kitchen.
138 pages • 5½ x 8¼ • 0-7818-0765-4 • $22.50hc • (543)

All prices subject to change without prior notice. **To purchase Hippocrene Books** contact your local bookstore, call (718) 454-2366, or write to: HIPPOCRENE BOOKS, 171 Madison Avenue, New York, NY 10016. Please enclose check or money order, adding $5.00 shipping (UPS) for the first book and $.50 for each additional book.